T0199199

ACCESSING
THE
Scriptures
THROUGH STUDY AND PRAYER

The King Is Coming
TWO BIBLE WORK STUDIES
FOR - INDIVIDUALS - COUPLES - GROUPS

THE PROPHESIES OF
THE BOOK OF DANIEL
THE BOOK OF REVELATION

JOHN PENNINGTON
LARGE PRINT BIBLE STUDIES

WESTBOW
PRESS®
A DIVISION OF THOMAS NELSON
& ZONDERVAN

Copyright © 2016 John Pennington.
Earth Photo by Gene Cernan available by National Aeronautics and Space Administration.
Hand sketches by Kieran Seitz

All rights reserved. No part of this book may be used or reproduced by any means, graphic, electronic, or mechanical, including photocopying, recording, taping or by any information storage retrieval system without the written permission of the author except in the case of brief quotations embodied in critical articles and reviews.

This book is a work of non-fiction. Unless otherwise noted, the author and the publisher make no explicit guarantees as to the accuracy of the information contained in this book and in some cases, names of people and places have been altered to protect their privacy.

WestBow Press books may be ordered through booksellers or by contacting:

WestBow Press
A Division of Thomas Nelson & Zondervan
1663 Liberty Drive
Bloomington, IN 47403
www.westbowpress.com
1 (866) 928-1240

Andrew Murray - 199 Treasures of Wisdom on Talking with God used by permission of Barbour Publishing, Inc.

Poh Fang Chia, Our Daily Bread, © 2015 by Our Daily Bread Ministries, Grand Rapids, Michigan. Used by permission. All rights reserved.

Bibles
New International Version Fully Revised Copyright 1985, 1995, 2002 Zondervan
New King James Version 2nd Edition Copyright 1997, 2007 Thomas Nelson
Life Application Study Bible NIV Copyright by Tyndale House and Zondervan
The Narrated Bible Chronological Copyright secured from Zondervan by Harvest House
The Amplified Bible Eighteenth Printing 1979 Zondervan

Commentaries
Thru The Bible J. Vernon McGee Thomas Nelson
The Bible Exposition Commentary/Prophets Warren W. Wiersbe Victor/Cook
The Bible Exposition Commentary/New Testament Vol. 2 Warren W. Wiersbe Victor/Cook
The MacArthur Bible Commentary, Unleashing God's Truth, One Verse At A Time
Copyright 2005 by John MacArthur, Printed by Thomas Nelson
Heaven Randy Alcorn

Because of the dynamic nature of the Internet, any web addresses or links contained in this book may have changed since publication and may no longer be valid. The views expressed in this work are solely those of the author and do not necessarily reflect the views of the publisher, and the publisher hereby disclaims any responsibility for them.

Any people depicted in stock imagery provided by Thinkstock are models, and such images are being used for illustrative purposes only.
Certain stock imagery © Thinkstock.

ISBN: 978-1-5127-2240-6 (sc)
ISBN: 978-1-5127-2239-0 (e)

Library of Congress Control Number: 2015920158

Print information available on the last page.

WestBow Press rev. date: 02/24/2016

In Memory of Bob Jefferson

CONTENTS

Twelve Lessons The Book of Daniel

Twenty One Lessons The Book of Revelation

FROM THE AUTHOR

Upon receiving a Music Education Degree in 1959, my university advisor advised me not to teach because I was not the teacher type. As providence would have it, I taught public school music thirty-five years! This was God's way to prepare me to teach His Word. There was a problem, I never had a Bible nor attended church.

Being the product of an environment that cursed church and Jews alike pretty much sums up my early development. Fortunately, Christ was introduced to me by a Boy Scout leader. At age seventeen, an armed standoff with an enraged stepfather drove me from home. By God's grace, I was given the gift of music which gave me the means to sustain my family. I eventually did attend church but never stepped foot in any system of Bible study. It simply would be too embarrassing; my biblical illiteracy would be exposed. I did hear many a good sermon but never wrote anything down. Sermons enforced my sense of morality and that Jesus saves but still, I was totally unaware the Bible had sections. Worse, I thought NIV was a medical term.

"Come to me, all you who are weary and burdened, and I will give you rest." I once would have said this was about working three jobs. A Bible study class provided me keys to identify this verse as freedom from any form of religious straight-jacket.

It is a joyful delight to become biblically literate. Being a believer and biblically illiterate is very unsettling. Believe me, a great deal of leg work was required in the dozen years of creating Bible studies. Oh how I have loved every minute of it! Connecting the dots and discovering the depths of the Creator of all things became a passion. I thank God my lone A in the ninth-grade was typing. Becoming biblically literate is like a breath of fresh air. The more you know of God working in the lives of men, nations and prophecy, the more you will come to treasure the Savior.

The backdrop of these studies are the result of being AARP eligible. My wife and I were drawn into senior community living. From the beginning, we planned to form a community within the community by starting a Bible study. Considering people have little in common except gravity and geography, the power in the name Jesus was the best path to assemble a group of like-minded people. It would be these folks with whom we would enjoy residential association for years to come. The first group was launched in 2005 and a second followed in 2012. In addition to class, the groups enjoy Christmas banquets and other social functions. My wife and I have in fact, taken some of our class-members water skiing.

LOOK IT UP! WRITE IT DOWN!

I spoke of hearing marvelous sermons yet remained biblically illiterate. All of us learned core subjects such as grammar, math, history and biology by means of a pencil and a workbook. I believe heavily, a workbook in combination with an overview is superior to lecture alone. There is no substitute for cementing information than to <u>look it up</u> and <u>write it down</u>! And, a workbook affords the opportunity for interactive discussion. It is amazing how much we learn from others.

Do older adults want to go back to school and prepare lessons? NO! Now you know why I prepare the workbooks we use. <u>The pedagogy, and this is important, for a residential Bible study *must fit* to keep the group returning year after year.</u> We briefly tried studies that provide answers in the back of the book but found they discouraged discussion and required little in the way of looking up related Scripture. Looking up Scripture is invaluable to discovering the geography of your Bible.

A pastor once told me, a study that does not require some page turning is too dumbed down to be of much value. Even though these studies are relatively brief, they require examining other parts of your Bible apart from the subject being studied.

NEVER CEASE LEARNING

"Ask and it will be given to you;
seek and you will find;
knock and the door will be opened to you."

This verse is my favorite to encourage people to attend a Bible study. Like piano lessons, weekly accountability pays dividends.

Some see this verse as relating to necessities. Others errantly relate the verse to God being a vending machine dispensing material goodies. For me, it is for God to open His Word up to me. Beloved, He has done this for me and our class members. They feel blessed when making new discoveries about God and about themselves.

As you study God's Word, do so with the intent to grow your relationship with your Lord and Savior. For certain, Bible study should never be viewed as a means to earn brownie points with God.

BE A TEACHER

"Do you understand what you are reading, Phillip asked?"
How can I, he said, unless someone explains it to me?"

Truly, none of us can pass on information we ourselves do not possess. A young believer often looks to an older believer for clarifications. We either give it to them or we know our way around the Bible to tell them where to look. If a skeptic asks why you believe in Jesus and you reply *'well I just do*, this is no witness to the lost! To them, faith and belief are foolishness. Skeptics need reasons and we need to give it to them! Faith is fitting when around other believers. But regarding the lost, we must *be equipped* to know why we have faith. If anyone ever told you faith is blind, they are wrong. Fulfilled prophecy is a reason to believe. Eyewitness accounts of the Apostles is another. Creation is yet another. The writers of the Bible were separated by centuries, yet all point to Christ. Isn't that just simply amazing? Absolutely, faith is on solid ground! To be an effective messenger of Christ requires the principles of 2 Timothy 4:2 and 1 Peter 3:15.

AND FINALLY

Life's path takes many turns. If God wishes to use you, sometimes He will relocate you. There are numerous examples in Scripture where God relocated His servants. My path to biblical literacy and therefore usefulness to God *was* a matter of geography, literally. It began with meeting my wife Mary in Albuquerque, New Mexico. She gave me a leather-bound Bible. It was my first. What an amazing gift to receive! Now possessing my own Bible with my name imprinted on its cover, I was charged! I cannot describe the feeling of seeing my name inscribed on the cover of that Bible.

It was as if I were actually viewing my name written in the Lamb's Book of Life! But who would teach me? I was as the Ethiopian of Acts Eight, who needed a Phillip to get him up to speed. God responded to my willingness to learn. To God be the glory! My Phillip was a godly man named Bob Jefferson, a learned lay leader and Teaching Director of a Community Bible Study, to whom this book is dedicated.

Give the gift of a Bible to someone.
Inscribe their name on it.
Some will be offended,
But no matter,
You may save a soul.

ACKNOWLEDGMENTS

For a Longsuffering Creator, full of Patience and generous of Grace. For Bob Jefferson, a godly man and gifted CBS Teaching Director whom God placed along my path. His tragic death in an automobile accident is still troublesome to understand. The men and women of Heritage Ranch and Villas in The Park communities of Fairview Texas who faithfully attended Tuesday night Bible study classes my wife and I established. And finally, my loving and supportive wife Mary, who literally forced me to attend a CBS Bible study while living in Albuquerque. Always at my side, she is the spark for every class. For the commentaries of gifted men and women whom God granted so much insight. And the Word itself, it is the teacher's teacher. Oh how it motivates those who assist others, such as Phillip in Acts 8, to better understand the faith and *why we believe!*

I mustn't forget music and all who make worship music available. Being a music person, we begin each class with music to set the tone from the toils of the day. We end each class singing "As We Go." A soft, gentle and beautiful way to end every class. This song is published by LifeWay Press.

These studies were prepared by a lay person for general enlightenment. They will not require the preparation time rigorous in depth studies demand...... John Pennington

Because of where Jesus is today, you have a hope for tomorrow

Jesus Is
Jesus is, God Invisible now seen by men.
Jesus is, Savior, Teacher, and Friend.
Jesus is, King of Kings and Lord of Lords.
Bow Thy Knee.

As Mary and I walked the stone paths of the Via De La Rosa in November 2013 we both remained quiet, at times tearful. We had just come from the Mount of Olives, the Garden of Gethsemane and entered Jerusalem's old city through the Joppa Gate. We had stood at the place where the night before He was crucified, Jesus prayed, anticipated, and resigned Himself to His mission and His purpose. In love, He would give Himself up for us, submitting to being nailed to a tree! By His sacrifice our sins are forgiven. Through Him, all who receive Him are forever reconciled to the Father.

With its shops and barking street vendors, the Via De La Rosa is quite different than in Jesus' day. To walk where Jesus walked is added strength to walk as Jesus taught. To love one another. Within the walls of the Church of the Holy Sepulcher one gets a surreal sense of what happened here. Events forever changing the world and the destiny of those who love the Lord above all. This is the First Commandment. If you have not studied about the Lord Jesus, do so without delay! He is your Savior, He is your Friend. Let Him also be your Teacher. He will teach you by the only means available, the Bible. If no Bible study is available, form one. Two or three people is all you need. Don't delay, bow thy knee, He is King of Kings and Lord of Lords.

"For God so loved the world that He gave His only Son. That who so ever would believe on Him shall have ever lasting life." (John 3:16)

HOW GREAT THOU ART

FOREWORD

From thirty-seven thousand miles away, Apollo 17 astronaut Eugene Cernan snapped this remarkable picture of the earth suspended in space. The picture affirms the words of the Apostle Paul; *"For since the creation of the world, God's invisible qualities - His eternal power and divine nature have been clearly seen."* In regard to the coming Judgment and unbelieving men, Paul writes; *"being understood from what has been made, men are without excuse."* Romans 1:20

From Cernan's photo it is inconceivable that a Creator is not behind such a fantastic physical fact. To believe the earth, its properties and the millions of life forms living on this celestial body are the result of random events requires far more faith than does believing a Creator exists. Can an atheist travel Cernan's path and still maintain there is no Creator? Assuredly he would have to be mad to view an earth suspended in space, surrounded by millions of celestial bodies and conclude all of this a random accident! *"Where were you when I laid the foundations of the earth?"*

As assuredly as God exists, would He not also communicate with those who were made in His Image? (Genesis 1:27) *"So God created man in His own image, in the image of God He created him; male and female He created them."* One would think that a Being who could create from nothingness all that is, men would hunger to hear what He has to say. Sadly, this is not the case. Many people are just too caught up with themselves to have any desire to have interest even in this Being who has put on display His Magnificence!

By your study of the Bible, you have said I acknowledge God is real and I want to know the mind of my Glorious Creator. For if I know His mind, I will surely better come to know Him.

One who loves the Lord is truly sanctified.
One who loves the Lord prays for wisdom, strength and vision.
He trusts God for every need, every decision.

THE BIBLE

This book contains the mind of God, the state of man, the way of Salvation, the doom of sinners, and the happiness of believers.

Its doctrines are holy, its precepts are binding, its histories are true, and its decisions are immutable.

Read it to be wise, believe in it to be safe, and practice it to be holy.

It contains light to direct you, food to support you and comfort to cheer you.

It is the traveler's map, the pilgrim's staff, the pilot's compass, the soldier's sword, and the Christian's charter.

Here paradise is restored, heaven opened, and the gates of hell disclosed.

Christ is its grand object; our good its design; and the glory of God, its end.

It should fill the memory, rule the heart, and guide the feet.

Read it slowly, frequently, and prayerfully.

It is a mine of wealth, a paradise of glory, and a river of pleasure.

It is given you in life, will be opened in the Judgment, and be remembered forever.

It involves the highest responsibility, will reward the greatest labor, and will condemn all who trifle with its sacred contents. Middletown Bible Church

Keys to Successful Study

Understand that from the story being told, a principal is being taught:

1. Identify and underline key verses.
2. Identify and circle key words.
3. Understand where and when the story takes place.
4. Picture yourself present!
5. Who is speaking and to whom?
6. What is the one speaking describing?
7. What or why is the person speaking?

Most mistakes for misunderstanding Scripture are due to not being aware of the context in which the speaker is referring to. It is always a good idea to examine preceding verses, even referring back to the beginning of a chapter if need be.

USING THESE STUDIES

These studies are designed for small groups of likeminded people meeting weekly at the same time and location. The large print makes them advantageous for senior communities. The lessons are also useful for individual, couple or family study and are easily understood by those with little to moderate knowledge of the Bible. If you have never attended a Bible study, these studies are for you!

Leading the studies is successful by one person or a couple. Leaders with limited preparation or knowledge should use the 'Helicopter Overview' provided following the discussion questions. For those living in a restricted community such as senior living or gated HOA, it is recommended a resident serve as leader. Non-resident leaders, even if Seminary trained are discouraged! The most well intended non-resident in time becomes inconsistent with outside conflicts as class after class is canceled. Soon, the group dissipates or a resident must step up and lead to save the class anyway. Do occasionally invite a Seminary trained guest speaker.

The studies were prepared by a lay person and can be led by an untrained believer willing to serve! Recall, not one Disciple Jesus called was qualified yet no one today disputes the statement of the Apostle's Creed. The Word is the real teacher! God didn't call the qualified, He qualified the called! God equips His people! These studies have been successfully tested using lay leaders for ten years. No one ever indicated anything other than, how much they had grown in their knowledge of God.

Rotating leaders is acceptable in the beginning until it is clear one person or a couple are gifted facilitators. Dependable leaders with people skills makes a class go. Ultimately, Scripture does the teaching!

The studies are drawn from the NIV Bible. In a class, read only the chapter being studied. [Also read aloud bracketed verses]. Reference verses apart from the study need not be read. Involve everyone in reading! To keep things moving, [bracketed verses] are best read by one person who has them located ahead of time. Occasionally you will find 'TIME OUT' sections that extend beyond the chapter being studied.

These studies are not intended to make one a biblical scholar but rather, to develop a loving relationship with Jesus. God's Grace in Christ is not fully appreciated until His Word is studied. If your lack of knowledge embarrasses you, get over it and get started! One day you will leave this life. Don't let that day descend on you without fully knowing your Lord and Savior. Know more today about Jesus then you knew yesterday. As your knowledge of Him increases, so shall your love for Him grow.

Twelve Lessons
The Book of

Daniel

Daniel ministered during the time of the Babylonian exile.

ABOUT DANIEL

The central challenge of Daniel lies in determining if passages are futuristic or if they have already occurred. Without over analysis, your study should consider <u>dual references</u> to both short and long term prophecy. Short term would include that time from Daniel to Christ. Long term reaching to end-times and the Second Coming of Christ.

Antiochus Epiphanes, a Greek king, did much of what Daniel prophesied, murdering Jews and erecting a pagan altar to Zeus on the sacred altar in the Temple of Jerusalem in 168 B.C.. And shortly after the time of Christ, the Romans razed Jerusalem destroying the Temple completely. However, based on the words of Christ in Matthew 24, it seems reasonable to accept the *"abomination that causes desolation"* of which Daniel speaks in Chapters eleven and twelve as futuristic. It is futuristic because of the context of Jesus' answer to His disciple's questions concerning His return to establish His Kingdom. To see a third Temple built seems improbable to us considering today's political conflicts in Jerusalem. Yet, God is Sovereign over men and nations, so it is not only possible, it is quite plausible this will come to pass.

The northern kingdom Israel had fallen to Assyria some one hundred twenty years earlier. With the southern kingdom Judah now fallen, God's Judgment upon the Jews was complete. Prophet after prophet had warned the Jews to give up idol worship and sinful living but their response was as always *"stiff necked!"*

Daniel begins in 605 B.C. when Babylon conquered Jerusalem and exiled young Daniel and his three youthful friends along with thousands. This exile of the Jews would last seventy years to the time the Persians would conquer Babylon. With God's involvement with people and nations, Daniel assumes the role of statesman by official appointment. He would spend his life as a confidante to kings and a prophet for both Babylonian and Persian empires. Daniel is confirmed as author of this book by Jesus in Matthew 24:15.

It would be from Babylon through Daniel that God would impart the stages of Gentile world domination down through the centuries. This Gentile domination would sustain until the coming Messiah would establish His Millennial Kingdom and again rescue His covenant people. These events foster in the *"time of the gentiles"* also called end-times. Some believe end-times began at the cross but Daniel supports a much earlier time line when Gentiles trampled the Holy City and Matthew 24 corroborates this. The cross event simply launched the Church age.

DANIEL 1
Trial, Trust, Faithfulness

At about age fifteen, Daniel finds himself whisked away to Babylon as a captive Hebrew. A crisis of conscience quickly ensues.

Read Daniel 1:1-2

1) Why would God be instrumental in Jerusalem falling to the Babylonians?
   [Read Jeremiah 25:8-11] See 2 Chronicles 15-21, Habakkuk 1:5-11

2) With the fall of Jerusalem, what new time line is established? See Luke 21:20-24

Read Daniel 1:3-14

3) Some of the captured Hebrews were to be pressed into becoming palace servants. Many qualities are listed for this service but one requirement is a must to even being admitted into training. What is it?

4) Why would age be so important to being selected to train as a servant?

5) What dietary foods would be required of Daniel that would violate his conscience? See Deuteronomy 14:3-21

Discussion:

   a) What standards today should Christians use in determining whether they should be a party to certain activities?

   b) When your biblical standards are challenged, do you place the same trust in God to see you through as did Daniel?

6) Which verse explains God's intervention on behalf of Daniel and the food he is required to eat?

7) What two verses tells of Daniel's trust that God will see him and his three companions through the dietary challenge?

Discussion:

Describe a time when you trusted God? What is your greatest trust you have placed in God? Is there a verse that affirms this trust? See John 19:30; Matthew 28:20; Hebrews 13:5

Read Daniel 1:15-21

8) Which verse tells us that Daniel's trust in God paid off?

Discussion:

How might verse seventeen relate to us today with regard to [Matthew 7:7-8]?

9) These four young men excelled in all aspects of their lives. When that occurs in a person in today's society, to whose credit is it usually given, the individual or God?

Discussion:

Did God simply want these four young men to have a good life in captivity or do you think He had further plans for them? See 2 Timothy 2:20-21

10) Daniel demonstrates a heart for God. What aspect of his character and conduct impresses you most?

11) What are ways today people can incorporate Daniel's character into the way they approach life? See Galatians 5:22; Ephesians 6:10-18

12) How do we know that Daniel would spend a lifetime in Exile?

13) Most know of God's miracle regarding Daniel in the lion's den. What are two less spectacular miracles God performed in Chapter 1?

Summary Statement:

Certainly Daniel did not intend to live his life in the court of a pagan king, yet, here he is! God's plans are not always as we would have them.

 **Leader's Helicopter Overview for Daniel 1**
(Optional or Prepare Your Own)

The Prophesy of Israel is fulfilled! God judges Judah and Jerusalem falls! Nebuchadnezzar, King of Babylon, lays siege to Jerusalem and the southern kingdom of Judah. (Northern kingdom Israel, fell years earlier to Assyria) Young Daniel and his three friends, being upper class Hebrews, are taken eight hundred miles away to be pressed into palace service of the Babylonian King, Nebuchadnezzar. As captives, they were to be retrained (brainwashed) to function in the pagan Babylonian society. Emasculation might also have occurred though scripture does not acknowledge such. The initial crisis was, to be forced to eat the Babylonian diet of foods forbidden for Jews.

Chapter 1 reveals the character of an individual who loves the Lord. Daniel, whose name means 'God is my Judge,' is a blue print for the character of a Christian! Believing and trusting God was a hallmark of Daniel's character and models how you and I are to live! God's faithfulness is observed as we see small but important miracles of God contribute to the success of Daniel and his three friends. The chief official, at his own risk, grants permission for Daniel to not be a party to the official diet. Result, mentally and physically, Daniel and his friends still emerge head and shoulders above the rest.

Question: In present day society, who is glorified when someone excels? What sin is this called?

Through God's intervention, our four young lads establish themselves as worthy to be chosen for royal positions in a foreign land. These positions will be a platform from which God will press them into His service.

Application

Keep godly values and trust God. *"He will never leave you or forsake you."* These young men might have concluded they had been wronged by their situation, blamed God and been tempted to sin by being rebellious. Had this been the case, Daniel and his friends would be useless to God. Consider these words of James.

"Consider it pure joy, my brothers, whenever you face trials of many kinds, because you know that the testing of your faith develops perseverance. Perseverance must finish its work so that you may be mature and complete, not lacking anything." James 1:2-3

God's plan may not be ours! <u>He wants patience to make its way into our character</u>. That we may become complete to do the work He sets before us. God had plans for Daniel and his friends and He has a plan for you!

Notes for Daniel 1

DANIEL 2
Crisis, Trust, Prophecy

Perplexed by dreams, Nebuchadnezzar creates another crisis for Daniel. With God's help, Daniel interprets the dreams, thus averting certain death for himself, his three friends and all of Babylon's servant fortune tellers.

Part I: Another Crisis - Read Daniel 2:1-18

1) Chapter 1 presents a crisis of conscience with the royal diet. What is the crisis here?

2) a. Rather than concocting a scheme to escape certain death, what is the first thing Daniel does? (v. 18)

   b. What does Daniel demonstrate to you in verse eighteen?

   c. Could you consider verse eighteen the central message of chapter two?

Discussion:

When a crisis occurs in life, generally what is the last thing people do? What is the first thing you do? What should be the first thing a believer should do when faced with a crisis?

3) How would you summarize the person and character of Nebuchadnezzar with specific attention to verse twelve?

Read Daniel 2:19-23

4) a. After reading these verses, how would you describe Daniel's relationship with God?

   b) This section of Daniel is Psalm like because it exalts God! Identify the numerous aspects of God's character that Daniel praises.

Read Daniel 24-49

5) As a result of Daniel's relationship with God, in what manner does Daniel approach the King's appointed assassin Arioch and Nebuchadnezzar?
   See Hebrews 4:16

Discussion:

Write down, memorize and recite with others [Philippians 4:13].

Part II Dream and Prophecy - Read Daniel 2:25-49

6) How is Daniel's answer to Nebuchadnezzar (vv.26-28a) different from the answer the servant fortune tellers gave the king in verse seven?

Discussion:

By human standards, Daniels audience with the king would be considered miraculous. Have there been times in your life something occurred that came across as divine?

7) What did Daniel want Nebuchadnezzar to learn about God? (vv. 27-30)

8) From head to toe, the metal in the statue degrades from a head of gold, to a body of silver, a bronze midsection, has legs of iron and the feet a mix of iron and clay. What conclusion might be drawn from this?

9) Verse forty-four is the bottom line of the prophecy. See Revelation 19:11-16 and explain how the prophecy of verse forty-four will be fulfilled.

Discussion:

From Nebuchadnezzar's response (vv. 46-47) was he converted or do you think he was simply recognizing the need to add a new god to his collection?

10) A relationship between a pagan king and a godly Jew is established. Compare the similarities and differences between Daniel and Joseph. See Genesis 40:1-23

Summary Statement:

Through a pagan king, God reveals a progression of empires and the return of a Christ who crushes His enemies and establishes His Kingdom on earth.

Nebuchadnezzar's Dream of a statue can be viewed in most Bibles.

Chapter two is one of the more prophetic chapters in all the Bible. It is an amazing testimony to the Sovereignty of God. From the image portrayed in chapter two, it is evident God is involved with nations, a long term program for Israel and the unfolding human story in general. Today we know that many of these empires have risen and fallen. Such is the testimony to how temporary is the state of unstable men. Not until Christ returns will stability be set into place. Though the subject of heaven is not addressed here, this chapter alone makes it apparent heaven is going to be on earth which would put its counterpart just under our feet.

Not only does Daniel interpret Nebuchadnezzar's dream, he even describes the dream without the king telling him. Daniel's narrative was indeed spectacular. Nonetheless, <u>Daniel quickly gives credit to God</u>. As a result, the Spirit of God having worked through Daniel allows him and his three friends to escape certain death along with a score of undeserving fortunetellers. This is testimony that a single godly man can be instrumental in the deliverance of people. For other examples of godly men delivering people from death see: Acts 27:18-24, Jonah 1:11-16

<u>A relationship between a pagan leader and a godly man is established.</u> Sadly, this lesson escapes most Christian leaders today! Because of the infiltration of politics into the Church, who She seems to serve is getting a bit fuzzy. Burning bridges has become preferable to building them. The result, Satan has successfully created a divide even among believers. What Daniel accomplished in his time is impossible today. Even more remarkable is Daniel's unusual relationship with a pagan king. Daniel, a Jew, suggests his three Jewish friends be appointed to high positions of authority in Babylonian society.

Application

<u>Boldly trust God</u>! God is at work in the world! Therefore, to worry is to sin. For worry suggests God cannot be trusted. God is at work, even now, to bring our world to the conclusion prophesied in Revelation 19:11 - 22:21. Maranatha!

Notes for Daniel 2

DANIEL 3
A Testing of Faith

There are times in life when we are pulled in two different directions? Such is the case in this chapter. Daniel is absent, but his three friends make the right choices when their faith is put to the test.

Read Daniel 3:1-7

1) Compare the similarities of Daniel 3:4-7 and Revelation 13:14-15.

2) The devil tempts us to set-aside or even destroy our faith. God's trials are employed to test and strengthen our faith. Do you think Daniel 3:4-7 is the devil's attempt to destroy faith or do you think God is testing faith?

Discussion:

When trials come, how can we know if it is Satan's flaming arrows or God strengthening our resolve to remain faithful? Read Matthew 4:1-11

3) With a strong emphasis on music in these verses, do you think the music presented appealed to a Spirit of worship or was it music to excite the flesh?

Discussion:

What do you think is the state of music in today's Church?

Read Daniel 3:8-23

4) Why are we to obey civil authority? See Romans 13:1-7, Titus 3:1

5) In what situations should Christians disobey civil authority?
   See Matthew 22:15-21, Acts 5:27-29

6) According to vv. 16-18, what were Shadrach, Meshach and Abednego

    a. certain of?

    b. uncertain of?

7) How does the faith of these three young men compare with Daniel?

8) Circle and count how many times *"worship"* appears in Chapter three.

Discussion:
Shadrach, Meshach and Abednego were in a dire situation. Certainly sin can put us into bad situations. But what do you say to Christians who believe that all problems are the result of sin?

Read Daniel 3:24-30
9) How did God comfort these three young men during their time inside this fire?

Discussion:
You may not have ever been inside a fire, but do you recall a time when you faced a trial that was not the result of sin? What was the issue and why do you think you experienced it?

10) a. Describe the king's reaction when the young men did not perish.

    b. Why was his reaction predictable? See Romans 14:11, Isaiah 45:23

Summary Statement:
An idol doesn't have to be a statue. An idol is anything that moves God to a second place position in a person's life. Undoubtedly, Jews were among the people who took the easy way and *"fell down and worshiped the image of gold."* The fourth figure in the fire demonstrates God is ever present with His people.

Accessing the Scriptures

God often uses ungodly men to accomplish His purpose. God hardened Pharaoh's heart to serve a purpose. *"I will harden Pharaoh's heart."* (Exodus 7: 3) Nebuchadnezzar was God's instrument in Judgment on the nation Israel. In this chapter, a pagan king is used to test and separate persons who do not put God in first place. It foretells John the Baptist's prophecy of the Second Coming. *"His winnowing fork is in His hand, He will clear His threshing floor, gathering His wheat into the barn and burning up the chaff with unquenchable fire."* (Matthew 3:12)

Like much of Daniel, this chapter is highly prophetic. Daniel's absence say some, represents the absence of a raptured Church in the coming Tribulation. The three boys represent God protecting His remnant during the Tribulation.

Give close attention to these: Nebuchadnezzar displays characteristics of the beast out of the sea in Revelation 13:1-8. As king of the empire, he insists people of all nations, (Nebuchadnezzar ruled over all nations of that ancient world) worship both himself and his ridiculous statue (Satan). Second, the fire the three boys are in is without a doubt, prophetic of the judgment of a man's works. *"And the fire will test the quality of each man's work"* It is also symbolic of Eternal Judgment. *"It is appointed for men to die once, after this the judgment."* (Hebrews 9:27 NKJV) Scripture assures us testing will be by fire. There should be no speculation who is the fourth Being in the fire.

Shadrach, Meshach and Abednego were saved from the fire of Judgment! Beloved, He will save you! If you haven't taken the Lord Jesus into your life, do so now. Where you sit, trust in the Lord Jesus at this very moment.

His love will never let you go. On this promise you may rest well dearly beloved.

In thanksgiving, give back the life you now owe, sanctified by Him, let all men know.

You don't have to wait on the availability of a water Baptism. Like the thief on the cross, He is calling you. Believe and be saved! Pray this prayer.

Lord, come into my life. I know you died for me and rose again. You freely gave yourself up for me as a gift and I accept. Thank you sweet Jesus. Amen

Application

What choices do you make when you are pulled in two different directions? Do you choose the way that is expedient or as these boys, 'Put God First?' *"As for me and my house, we will serve the Lord."* (Joshua 24:15) As assuredly as you breathe, God tests you! How are you measuring up?

Notes for Daniel 3

DANIEL 4
Sovereignty - God is in Control

The most powerful emperor on earth was no match for God! In chapter one, God had delivered Jerusalem to Nebuchadnezzar. Then God took away his kingdom, even his humanity and then restored all of it back to him again.

With the aid of a dictionary, write the definition of *Sovereign*.

If you are not familiar with the term Eschatology, look this up also.

Read Daniel 4:1-3

1) a. How different is Nebuchadnezzar's praise of God here from his praise in Daniel 3:28-29? (after the furnace event)

    b. Do you see a difference in the King's character and personality?

Discussion:

When people receive Christ, what changes do you observe in them?

Read Daniel 4:4-18 - Dream of a Tree

2) a. Describe the tree (vv. 11-12)

    b. What was so shocking to Nebuchadnezzar? (vv.13-14)

3) What was the king of Heaven's message to this king on the earth?
    See vv. 17, 25, 32

Discussion:

What do you say about anyone who orders the destruction of something that is beautiful as well as useful? What does God say? See Isaiah 55:8-9

4) Why do you think God was so intent with impressing this king with His absolute authority instead of His Grace or His Love?

5) What is the end plan of God for earth and how will His plan come about?
See 2 Peter 3:10-13

Discussion:
If verse seventeen is applicable today, we therefore must assume that Hitler, Stalin and all evil leaders come into power by God's decree? Why might this be?

Discussion:
If God allows evil leaders, is your perception of God challenged?

Read Daniel 4:19-27 - Daniel Interprets the Dream
Author's Assistance - Verses 24-27 has to do with the King putting off repenting and forcing God's hand in Judgment. The stump and its roots being allowed to remain reminds us that God can see into the future. Nebuchadnezzar would repent and God would restore him.

6) Write a sentence that you believe explains repentance as God views it.

Read Daniel 4:28-37
7) What characteristic of God moved Him to wait twelve months before executing Judgment on King Nebuchadnezzar? (v. 29)

8) Power and pride go hand in hand. Compare Nebuchadnezzar with King Herod. Include the outcome of each. See Acts 12:20-23

Discussion:
In regard to Daniel speaking truth to hard hearts, what are some of the potential risks?
See Matthew 14:3-4

9) Draw a simple comparison between vv. 36-37 with the Parable of the Prodigal Son. See Luke 15:21-24

Summary Statement:
God remains Supreme. All mankind are His subjects. When men glorify themselves and ignore their Creator, they are in danger of descending to the level of animals. See Revelation 14:9-11

The Sovereignty of God over men and nations is the principal subject here. Buried in the Bible is this significant chapter on just how far reaching God's Sovereignty is. This chapter is not about Nebuchadnezzar's dream, Daniel's interpretations or the King's mental state. Prophecy not with-standing, the Sovereignty of God is this chapter's focal point. It is here to help men fully understand God controls men and nations, the rise and fall of them and the conditions present for restoration. <u>This translates into trust!</u> Christians are to have confidence in every presidential election knowing God is in control. Like it or not, His man is in the white house! <u>He may or may not be a godly man but he is God's choice</u> to accomplish a Divine Purpose.

Question: How much of a roll do you think Hitler had in the establishment of the Jewish State, Israel in 1948?

Some years have passed between chapter three and chapter four. Nebuchadnezzar is now giving an account of his personal experience during those years. His account of his seven year tribulation is amazing. One would think he was so out of it during that time he would have no recollection of any of it. Obviously, God left him with enough memory intact that he wouldn't soon forget the experience.

Question: Why do you think God removed Nebuchadnezzar's humanity and his kingdom but left him with his memory?

After the seven years, this once arrogant, narcissistic king must have been unrecognizable to those who had known his old self. Only God can change a man that much! To God be the glory! The stump and its roots could have been destroyed by the avenger angel, yet the stump is spared the destruction it deserved. The tree image is Nebuchadnezzar and the stump is his empire. After the king's seven year tribulation, the empire comes back even more magnificent than before. God was indeed gracious. This will be true of earth one day also! By leaving the stump and the roots, God gave us a look into the future. This tells us of the future following the Great Tribulation. A future that will usher in a new, more Glorious Kingdom, void of the Nebuchadnezzar narcissistic types, and replaced by a new kind of man!

<u>Application</u>

<u>Be confident, God is in control!</u> No matter how bad the world becomes, we can be confident that everything is moving according to God's End Plan. If the world was just wonderful and becoming godlier, Christ would need never return!

Notes for Daniel 4

DANIEL 5
A Prophecy is Fulfilled

Time passes, Daniel is up in years. Kings have come and gone but Daniel remains available for God to use again. This time, to usher in the second stage of the prophecy of Nebuchadnezzar's statue dream. The rise and fall of empires.

Read Daniel 5:1-7

1) Reread Daniel 1:2 and 2:2 and describe the character similarities of King Belshazzar and King Nebuchadnezzar.

2) Compare Belshazzar's emotions in verses five through seven with the emotions of Nebuchadnezzar's in Daniel 4:4-5.

3) How did these two pagan Kings respond to their fears?

Discussion:

What are things people do today when they are afraid of unexplained occurrences?

Personal question: Have you ever sought out a palm reader or tarot card reader for advice? If so, how long did this continue? Is your life governed in any way from reading your personal horoscope in newspapers or magazines?

4) What would you advise a friend who uses astrology and other forms of physic activities for guidance?

Read Daniel 5:8-17

5) What is Daniel's reputation?

Discussion:

Reputation follows everyone. So what establishes the reputation of each one of us? *"Let your light shine before men, that they may see your good deeds and praise your Father in heaven."* Matthew. 5:16

'Don't shine so others can see you. Shine so that through you others can see Him.'

- C.S. Lewis

Time out Discussion: Sometimes, ruined reputations are not self-inflicted. In our modern society, reputations can be destroyed by *character assassins.*

    a. In politics, what is the motive of a character assassin?

    b. In marriage with children, what is the motive of a spousal character assassin?

    c. Socially and in business, what is the motive of a character assassin?

i)   Identify some of the sins of a character assassin. Are you a character assassin?

ii)   Daniel had established a reputation among unbelievers! How does a Christian establish a reputation among unbelievers?

Using a dictionary, define Empathy.

Read Daniel 5:18-30 - Read Ezekiel: 21:27 from Amplified Bible - Zondervan

6)   What significant insight did Daniel give Belshazzar? (v.20)

7)   In a word, why was Lucifer deposed out of heaven? See Isaiah 14:12-14

8)   What is the message of Matthew 5:5?

9)   Nebuchadnezzar and Belshazzar had much in common in their early lives. How did God deal differently with these two pagan kings?

10) What does this say about the Sovereignty of God? See Romans 9:1-16

Brain Teaser:

What does verse twenty nine suggest about Belshazzar's leadership position as a Babylonian Monarch?

Summary Statement:

That means God's word is trustworthy because He is in control!

Daniel's summons to Belshazzar to interpret the king's dreams is similar to Nebuchadnezzar's summons for the same reason.

The sudden appearance of King Belshazzar is not such a jolt if we keep in mind The Book of Daniel has stops and starts that account for sixty-plus years. Numerous monarchs have come and gone during this period. Belshazzar is the last Babylonian. The Bible's use of the term father in verse two should not be taken literally as in that time, one who follows in a generational line was considered a son. Meaning they had the right of inheritance. I.e. Christians are all called sons of Abraham. Biblically this has to do with inheritance.

It is not the purpose of this study to work through the progression of Babylonian monarchs other than to note, none of them had the lengthy run of Nebuchadnezzar. Daniel's relationship with King Nebuchadnezzar had served to make his life secure and probably routine. Given Daniel's faith during his youth and in this chapter, it is easy to assume he remained faithful to God throughout his life. Most likely he ministered to other exiled Jews during these years.

Historically, the events here took place in 539 B.C.. Babylonians believed their city impregnable. But the Medo-Persian army commanded by Cyrus the Great proved otherwise. Babylon fell that very evening, thus fulfilling Daniel's prophecy.
See Daniel 2:39a.

Chapter five again confirms God's Sovereignty as we see one empire swiftly fall and another rise. Daniel's interpretation of Nebuchadnezzar's dream prophesied the fall of Babylon. That prophecy was fulfilled in this chapter.

Application

Be a Daniel. Even into our later years, never outgrow being available for God's use. The self-confident, the proud, the arrogant and all who ignore the one and true living God Scripture puts on notice that God's Judgment can come swiftly. There is this Commandment! *"You shall have no other God's before Me!"* The result of not putting <u>God in first place</u> is illustrated in this chapter.

Jesus used hyperbole to get across the point that He is to have first position on one's life. *"If anyone comes to me and does not hate his father and mother, his wife and children, his brothers and sisters - yes, even his own life - he cannot be my disciple."* (Luke 14:26)

Notes for Daniel 5

DANIEL 6
Deja-Vu All Over Again

Chapter three and six are much the same. The players and manner of death are different but both chapters focus on God testing and protecting His people.

Read Daniel 6:1-5
1) Why do the Babylonian administrators vehemently resent Daniel?

Discussion:
Have you seen examples of this in the work place? What was the end result for the victim?

2) What verse identifies Daniel as a godly man? _____

Read Daniel 6:6-14 - Plot against Daniel
3) Recall, verse six records what was a common greeting to Nebuchadnezzar and to Belshazzar. To what sinful nature did this form of greeting play to? See Proverb 16:18

Discussion:
In what arenas of our society is defamation of character the norm? In the end when God judges, who will be the greater loser? See Daniel 6:24

Discussion:
Has there been instances in your life others set out to discredit you unjustly? What do you think motivated these attacks on your character or abilities?

4) What is the decree that Darius signs?

5) What was Daniel's response to being forced to worship Darius as a God?

6) What was Daniel asking of God? (v. 11)

7) Read Genesis 37:1-28 and compare the brothers of Joseph with those who plot against Daniel.

8) Describe Darius' emotions upon receiving accusations against Daniel?

Read Daniel 6:15-22

9) a. What was the emotional state of the king lying in his bed during the night while Daniel spent the night in a den of Lions?

   b. Who had the more restful night? Why?

Read Daniel 6:23-28

10) God spared Daniel from being killed by the lions. When was another time God spared one of His own death by a lethal creature? See Acts 28:5

Personal Thought:

When good things happen for others, are you envious or are you joyful?

11) What does the Bible say why there was not a scratch on Daniel? (v. 23)

12) Compare King Darius' final testimony (vv. 25-27) with the final testimony of King Nebuchadnezzar. See Daniel 4:34-35

13) What do the testimonies of the two kings reveal about God?

Discussion:

Read Revelation 13:15-18 and discuss when antichrist and his false prophet come on the world scene, what do you think most people will do and why will they do it?

Summary Statement:

Daniel's restoration to authority is met with a plot to destroy him. But God was as close as Daniel's knees. As with Daniel, prayer was also the essence of Jesus' relationship with the Father. See Mark 14:12-36

The head of gold (Babylonian Empire) has been replaced by the chest and arms of silver. (Medo-Persia Empire) This period would continue roughly two hundred years. Eventually it too would decline and be replaced by the Greek Empire of Alexander the Great. (Belly and Thighs of Bronze) It is worthy to note, during the Persian domination, Jews were allowed a return to Jerusalem where Nehemiah would oversee restoration of the city including its walls.

Whether or not the accounts of Chapter six points to the Great Tribulation, it must be considered. Decidedly, it is important the faithfulness of both God and Daniel is observed. With a Persian king governing, Daniel's position of authority is restored. It seems likely that Daniel had slipped into obscurity following the years of King Nebuchadnezzar's reign. Now back on the scene and given a high position of authority once again, others plot to see the last of him. Their plot is fated to failure because they do not accept the Sovereignty of God. *"If God is for us, who can be against us?"* (Romans 8:31) Like all men who dismiss the might of God, in the end, they reap death. For Belshazzar, his destruction came swiftly when he least expected it!

"For the Lord loves justice; He will not forsake His saints.
They are preserved forever. But the descendants of the wicked shall be cut off"
Psalm 37:28-29 (NKJV)

Idea Exchange:
Daniel and his friends are miraculously spared! Others such as John the Baptist (Matthew 14:10-11) and Stephen (Acts 7:59) are not! How is God glorified by the miraculous survival of some and martyrdom of others?

"You and I live in a lion's cage. That cage is the world, and there is a big roaring lion prowling up and down the cage. Peter calls him our adversary, the Devil." *

Application

Daniel was not thrown into the den of lions for sinning, but for being a godly man. This chapter is a classic example of the human heart when it is not controlled by the Holy Spirit. Have you ever been guilty of acting against or demeaning another person when you knew in your heart you were not justified? Did you feel satisfaction or regret? This chapter concludes historic Daniel. Take time to reflect back on God at work in the lives of believers, unbelievers and His Sovereignty over nations.

*Taken from, Through the Bible Commentary Series - J. Vernon McGee Copyright 1975, 1991 Used by permission of Thomas Nelson www.thomasnelson.com All Rights Reserved

Notes for Daniel 6

AN URGENT MESSAGE

A Closing Door

Beep, beep, beep, beep. The warning sound and flashing lights alerted commuters the train door was about to close. Yet a few tardy individuals still make a frenzied scramble across the platform and onto the train. The door closed on one of them. Thankfully it rebounded and the passenger boarded the train safely. I wondered why people took such risks when the next train would arrive in a mere 4 minutes.

There is a far more important door that we must enter before it closes. It is the door of God's mercy. The apostle Paul tells us, *"Behold, now is the accepted time; behold now is the day of salvation"* (2 Corinthians. 6:2). Christ has come, died for our sins, and has risen from the grave. He has opened the way for us to be reconciled to God and has proclaimed for us the day of salvation.

Today is that day. One day the door of mercy will close. To those who received and served Christ, He will say, *"Come, you blessed of my Father, inherit the kingdom prepared for you"* (Matthew 25:34). But those who don't know Him will be turned away (Luke 13:25).

Our response to Jesus Christ determines our destiny! Today Jesus invites.
"I am the door. If anyone enters by Me, he will be saved." **(John 10:9)**

Today the gate is open,
And all who enter in
Shall find a Father's welcome,
And pardon for their sin.

There's no better day than today
to enter into God's family.

A Closing Door - Poh Fang Chia, Our Daily Bread®, ©2015 Reprinted by Our Daily Bread Ministries, Grand Rapids, MI. Reprinted by permission. All Rights Reserved.

At the conclusion of chapter four we see a redeemed Nebuchadnezzar. He confessed the one true God and was restored. That same restoration is available to all who confess Jesus Christ. On the other hand, at the conclusion of chapter five, we viewed a different fate for Belshazzar. He is swiftly cut off without remedy. Delay is deadly!

INDEX OF ILLUSTRATIONS FOR DANIEL 7 - 12

You have already experienced the use symbolism in the first six chapters. To assist your study going forward, use this page as a helpful reference.

Ancient of days:	God the Father
Bear & Ram	Medo - Persia (Iran)
Beast:	unflattering term for unregenerate man
Clouds of heaven	Christ's Return in Glory
Fire	Wrath/Judgment
Four winds	100% coverage, no place immune, no one can hide
Horn	ungodly power, nation, leader, institution or culture
Leopard & Goat	Greece
Little Horn	antichrist
Lion	Babylon (Iraq)
Fourth Beast	worldwide oppressor of the Jews and the saints (Rome or other, perhaps Babylon could be the secular world at large)
Northern King	Antiochus Epiphanes, foretells character of antichrist
Saints	Regenerated people-predestined by the Spirit thru Grace, not ballots.
Sea	The nations
Son of man	Jesus Christ
Times, times & a half time.	Forty-two months
White as snow:	Purity

As we enter this section of Daniel, let us be mindful that the study of prophecy should never be for the purpose to satisfy one's curiosity. Rather, the study of prophecy should be for the purpose of having a transforming effect upon our life.

DANIEL 7
Vision of Four Beasts and the Second Coming

The order your Bible presents the chapters is not in sequence with events as they occurred! I.e. Verse one reveals the events of Chapter seven occurred before Chapter five. Perhaps Daniel did not want to intermix his visions with other visions.

Numerous themes and details are presented in this chapter. Time will erase the particulars, but you can be confident, just as the saints are predestined, the fate of nations and unregenerate men is already recorded.

Read Daniel 7:1-8- Four Beasts

1) What is different about Daniel's dream experience here from his dream experience with Nebuchadnezzar in chapters two and four?

2) Who is the sitting king when Daniel has his vision of four beasts?

3) a. In our physical world, what causes the sea to churn violently?

   b. What might stormy weather suggest in regard to men and nations?

** Read Daniel 7:15-25

4) Revelation 13:1-2 *"And the dragon stood on the shore of the sea."* The dragon here is Satan! In Satan's cross hairs is every nation on earth! Perhaps he fantasizes all nations his kingdom and he has an earthly someone to assist him.

   a) Who is this fourth beast who will be Satan's number one man?

   b) How does the fourth beast exceed the first three? See Revelation 13:2

Discussion:
Verse twelve identifies betrayal. Verse twenty-five gives additional insight to betrayal. What is Daniel telling us in regard to the betrayals taking place?

** Read Daniel 7:9-14; 26-27 - Vision Of Ancient of Days

5) See Revelation 20:11-15 Compare Daniel's vision with John's vision six-hundred years later.

6) Verse ten reveals two very large groups present.

    a. Who is the group attending Him?

    b. Who is the group standing before Him?

    c. What is taking place? See Revelation 20:13

Discussion:

From Revelation 20:13 we read of people being judged by their own works! What does that tell you the choices they made regarding God's free gift of Grace?

7) The Son of Man is Jesus. What authority is Jesus given? See John 8:18

8) a. Reread vv. 9, 10 and 18. What hope are believers assured of?

    b. What do vv. 9-10, 18 mean to unbelievers? See 1 Corinthians 1:18

Summary Statement:

*Man views human kingdoms as valuable metals. (Chapter 2) God sees them as vicious animals, fighting and devouring one another. Human history will culminate in a world controlled by a satanic ruler. (antichrist) He will be a liar, betraying even his own. Jesus will end his boastful defiance of God!

*Taken from, Nelson's Quick Reference Bible Commentary - Warren W. Wiersbe Copyright 1991 Used by permission of Thomas Nelson www.thomasnelson.com All Rights Reserved
** Author's suggested reading and study order.

The altered order of verses for the study of this chapter is not intended to usurp Daniel's presentation, but rather to facilitate its reading and study. Readers certainly are free to follow the Bible's sequence.

The visions of beasts has to do with the *"time of the gentiles."* That time in history when Gentile nations dominate the world leading up to the Second Coming of Christ. The chapter also includes how those world systems end.

For us today, the time of the first three beasts have come and gone. (Reference your Bible's illustration of four beasts.) The Lion is Babylon, the Bear Medo-Persia. Both were part of Daniel's life. The Leopard and the Terrifying Beast would come after Daniel's time. For you and I, the Greek and Roman Empires are past, but like Nebuchadnezzar's stump, (Daniel 4:23) we anticipate a resurgence of First century Roman authority in the form of perhaps a European Union, or an ungodly world out of control. The Roman Church already has global influence and must have consideration producing the false prophet spoken of in John's Revelation.

Discussion questions:
Where might America fit into all this? Will America remain a protector of Israel? Will a future America join the Anti-Semitic world against Israel? With the absence of American protection, nations will surely come against Israel. Will that be the catalyst for Armageddon and the return of Christ?

Verse nine does its best to give a word picture of Mighty God. So let us say, our Magnificent Lord is indescribable! Daniel ends the chapter citing, he will keep his visions to himself. This will surface again in later chapters.

To borrow a saying from Solomon, *"a chasing after the wind."* While the beasts spend their waking hours warring to gain advantage over one another, God is in His heaven preparing to hold court! Jesus Christ will one day summon all mortals, living and dead to Judgment. After this, His Kingdom will come, His Will be done, <u>on earth</u> as it is in heaven!

<u>Application</u>
It is one thing to learn what Bible prophecy foretells in the future. But it is another thing to know what it means in our lives. With revelation comes responsibility! If we truly believe Christ is coming back to earth, how ought we to be?

Notes for Daniel 7

DANIEL 8
Vision of a Ram and a Goat

Until this chapter, Israel has not been a major player in Daniel. Beginning in chapter eight, Israel is front and center. It is not surprising earlier chapters two through seven were written in Aramaic. Hebrew language closes out the remaining chapters.

Read Daniel 8:1-14

1) The ram with two horns is later identified in verse twenty as two kings from Media and Persia. The length of the horn is used to illustrate longevity. To what might the verb *'charged'* illustrate?

2) Toward which direction is the ram charging? What direction is the goat charging? What is the end result when two forces charge toward each other?

3) Scripture uses the term animal to describe what kind of life style?

Note: The goat with a prominent horn is identified in verse twenty-one as Greece. The goat's prominent horn would be Alexander the Great. His death at an early age resulted in a four-way division of his empire. (v.8)

4) Who was the Jewish king whose kingdom was divided after his death?
   See 1 Kings 14:21

5) What would you say was the speed of the goat (Greeks) as it conquered all that stood before it?

6) What is being spoken of in verse fourteen that was so important to the Jews?
   See Daniel 9:21 and Exodus 29:38-39

Discussion

What sacraments does your church value? How personal are they to you? How would you react if those sacraments were no longer allowed?

Read Daniel 8:15-22

7) By this chapter, Daniel is up in years. In your own words, describe what you think would be Daniel's emotional state at this point in his life?

8) a. Who did God assign to explain Daniel's visions to him?
   See also Daniel 9:21

   b. Who was the angel God sent to announce John the Baptist?
   See Luke 1:11-13, 19

   c. Who was the angel God sent to announce Jesus? See Luke 1:26-31

Time Out: Why do you think the birth of Jesus was announced to shepherds in the field and not to the religious priests inside the City of Jerusalem?

Read Daniel 8:23-25

9) Gabriel is speaking here in terms of two evil individuals under Satan's control. Short term (200 yrs.) he is speaking of Antiochus Epiphanes. Long term he is speaking of antichrist. See Matthew 24:22-25

Note: See Overview for insight on Antiochus Epiphanes.

   a. Identify the holy people Antiochus Epiphanes would war against?

   b. Identify the holy people antichrist would war against?

   c. Describe the character of Antiochus and antichrist.

Read Daniel 8:26-27

10) What was Daniel's final instructions?

Discussion:

What did you find in this chapter was the most disturbing? What did you find comforting? Why do you think Daniel was instructed to keep quiet?

Summary Statement:

Not until Christ returns can peaceful men such as Daniel secure earthly peace.

Daniel's visions takes place from twenty-four to thirty-six months before they are initiated. Daniel envisions himself in a palace located next to a river in Susa. Susa was the cultural center of Persia, a city rivaling Babylon. Gabriel, one of the angels of the Lord, is assigned as Daniel's interpreter.

Time out: Angels play a significant role in Scripture. Take a few minutes and read Daniel 9:20-27, 10:13, 10:21, 12:1, Jude 9, Revelation 12:7-9. Note how these two angels are used and determine what their respective missions are.

Daniel's visions reveal a world at constant war with itself as cultures come against one another in the quest for dominance, power and wealth. Road rage is on the rise! It was fitting when the Psalmist wrote; *"the heathen rage"* (Psalm 2:1 NKJV). The nightly news will be reporting strife among people until Christ returns! Maranatha!

Understand, <u>verse nineteen is a lengthy time from the exile to Christ's return</u>! Relative to the Temple and the daily sacrifice of the Jews, (vv. 11-12) Antiochus Epiphanes, whose name means *god made manifest,* attempted to force the Greek culture on the Jews. (Circa 173 BC.) Antiochus' desired to complete the plan of Alexander the Great. This gave rise to the Maccabean struggle which we shall not enter into here. The intrusion of Antiochus into Jewish religious practices gave us the verse *"the abomination that causes desolation."* He placed an altar to Zeus in the Jerusalem Temple and forbidden animals were sacrificed at the altar of the Lord.

All of this may not seem important but actually it is! <u>Antichrist will be a repeat of Antiochus Epiphanes (little horn)</u>. When Jesus speaks of Daniel in Matthew 24:15 *"when you see standing in the holy place, the abomination that causes desolation",* He is speaking about a time during the seven year Tribulation leading up to His return. Here is where it gets complicated. Is Jesus indicating a third Temple will be built in Jerusalem or, is the Temple Jesus references one's body? Paul's letters refer to one's body as being a Temple of God. Given the political climate in Jerusalem, a third Temple seems highly unlikely. Yet let us not forget, God is in control!

Discussion:
Do you think a third Temple will be built at the temple mount site in Jerusalem?"

Application
"Sing to the Lord, praise His name" (Psalm 96:2) People will disagree concerning the details. But there can be no disagreement how amazing our God is! He orchestrates a program for Israel, for the raging nations and for the Church. Three programs working simultaneously to one grand ending!

Notes for Daniel 8

DANIEL 9
Prayer and Prophesy

One of the hallmarks of prayer in all the Bible is found here. Equally is the prophecy a hallmark on the subject. <u>Daniel's prayer and prophecy relates to Israel</u>. Daniel demonstrates the necessity to pray and to seek the Word.

Read Daniel 9:4-19

1) Without looking at a dictionary, write your definition of prayer?

2) Name as many benefits as you can think of a person receives when they pray.

Discussion:

On the subject of intercession and prayer see Hebrews 5:1-3, 7:24-28. In whose name should we pray and why?

3) From Daniel's prayer, identify as many elements as you can in his prayer.

4) a. How important do you think it is to understand the elements of prayer?

    b. What elements do you think the prayer of a Christian should include?

Praying in the Spirit appears three times in Scripture

"I will pray with my spirit, but I will also pray with my mind" 1 Corinthians 14:15
"Pray in the Spirit on all occasions with all kinds of prayers and requests" Eph. 6:18
"Build yourself up in your most holy faith and pray in the Holy Spirit" Jude 20

Discussion:

What does it mean to pray in the Spirit? See John 4:24 and Romans 8:26-27
Examine 1 Corinthians 14:1-19 and be prepared on the subject of tongues.

I must take time to come into God's presence,
To feel my weakness and my need,
And to renew my fellowship with Him *

* Taken from, 199 Treasures of Wisdom On Talking With God - Andrew Murray Copyright 2007. ISBN 978-1-59789-695-5
Used by permission of Barbour Publishing, Inc.

Read Daniel 9:1-3 and 9:20-27

5) Daniel was one to consult the Scriptures. What words of encouragement would he have found in Jeremiah? See Jeremiah 29:10-14

6) Who appeared while Daniel was praying?

7) What was the reason given why Daniel's prayer was answered quickly?

8) After God used pagan Babylon to serve his purpose, what would be Babylon's fate? See Jeremiah 25:11-14

<u>Author's assistance pertaining to the time line of vv. 24-27</u>:

"Seventy sevens" (v. 24) represents the program for Israel. This is centuries and still counting until the Second Coming of Christ. This time period is in three segments:

i) In seven weeks (49 years) Cyrus the Great (Ezra 1:1-4) would issue a decree to allow Jews to return to Jerusalem and rebuild. (538 B.C.) See 2 Chronicles 36:22-23

ii) After sixty-two weeks (434 years) with the start of Jesus' ministry, perhaps extending to the Roman destruction of Jerusalem 70 A.D. and the Diaspora that followed.

Time out: Program for Israel now on hold as biblical history enters into the Church age.

iii) One week (7 years) restarts program for Israel. *"Time of Jacob's trouble"* [Read Jeremiah 30:7-10] Corresponds with Revelation 6-19 {Tribulation}.

9) a. Who is the he mentioned three times in verse twenty seven? (Revelation 13:1-2)

   b. What will this individual do?

   c. What will be his end? (Revelation 19:20)

Summary Statement:
For Daniel, prayer and studying Scripture were inseparable in his walk of faith.

Prayer was as much a part of Daniel's life as was food and drink. Daniel's prayer was not haphazard or as if standing before a vending machine, but is delivered with great respect for who God is. Too often our prayers are so focused on wants and needs of self and others <u>we forget the magnificence of the One to Whom we pray</u>!

Daniel's prayer is recorded for one reason, for you and me. We need to know how God wants us to pray. You can tell if a person is praying in the Spirit or not. If their prayer is me centered and in no way glorifies God if answered, rest assured, such a prayer is not in the Spirit! [See 1 Corinthians 14:15, Ephesians 6:18, Jude 20] Daniel's prayer acknowledges God for who He is and what He has done. God already knows who He is and what He has done in your life, <u>but He wants to hear it from you</u>. Much like a spouse knows you love them but they want to hear you say it. Not for them, *but for what it does for you*!

Daniel acknowledges both himself and his people as sinners and deserving of Judgment. His prayer reveals anguish and emotion of a repentant soul pleading for mercy both for himself and for his people. <u>Recheck question three, did you include anguish and emotion in your answer?</u> Daniel petitions God to restore Jerusalem and the Temple. Ironically, contrary to man's way, <u>God is glorified not by everlasting punishment, but by everlasting Mercy!</u>

Application

Greatness is not revealed by how justified you are when you punish those who have wronged you. <u>Greatness is revealed in how merciful you are in your forgiveness</u>!

Sin is a word modern society doesn't embrace, but <u>sin is the reason men and nations one day face Judgment</u>. In chapters such as this, God reveals His program for Israel, the nations and the Church for one reason. He is glorified by the Mercy He will grant to those who accept His Mercy. They are those who will listen, heed the warnings and prepare. (Revelation 2-3) Daniel's prophecy is like a road sign warning; 'bridge out ahead, no thru traffic, turn right here, continue your journey.' Beloved, if you haven't taken the new route to continue living beyond this life, do so now.

<u>Recommended books on prayer</u>:
Praying the Prayers of the Bible by James Banks, the Lost Art of Praying Together & Prayers for Prodigals by James Banks – Discovery House Publishers

Notes for Daniel 9

DANIEL 10
Two Visitors

In retrospect, this chapter is Daniel's account of circumstances surrounding the visions made known to him in Chapters eleven and twelve.

Read Daniel 10:1-9

1) Daniel describes his actions surrounding his receiving revelation from God. If you were in Daniel's shoes, what things would be running through your mind?

2) Chrysolite (v.6) is one of the terms used here to describe one individual. The word does not appear in Webster, but it appears in the Bible. What might the word Chrysolite relate to? See Revelation 21:2, 21:20

3) Daniel's vision of a man had a *"voice like a multitude."*(v.6) What might this suggest about who this man is? See Nehemiah 1:9, Revelation 19:6

4) Compare Daniel's experience (vv. 4-8a) with the Apostle Paul's experience on the road to Damascus. See Acts 9:3-7

Discussion:
Verse eight ends with *"I was helpless."* Verse ten begins with *"A hand touched me."* Recall a time of helplessness, but then you felt a hand of comfort come over you.

Personal Reflection:
Praying with other believers is a wonderful thing. But don't let it be the only time you engage prayer. There is no greater Communion with God than time spent alone with Him.

Read Daniel 10:10-15

5) How does verses ten and eleven lead us to believe that a second person, different from the first person, is speaking to Daniel?

6) What is on-going in the spiritual realm that would explain one of God's messengers being delayed in coming to Daniel? See Ephesians 6:12; Revelation 12:7

7) If God's messengers can be delayed, do you think it is also possible that delay to a prayer being answered is possible for the same reason?

8) Do you believe demons exists?

Time out: Do demons really exist? Certainly, sophisticated society doesn't recognize them. Ephesians 6:10-12 not only implies the existence of demons, it takes them for granted! If we believe the accounts of Jesus, His life and His ministry, neither angels nor demons can be ignored. An angel announced the birth of Jesus! Jesus had numerous contacts with demons! There are many references to demons even in the New Testament. Demons have names and engage in conversation. They display intelligence, emotions and will. Originally, demons were created angels, neither reproducing nor dying. They were given a freewill. Those who rebelled against God found their way into Satan's service.

Discussion:
What might be some reasons prayers are not answered or, are not answered right away?

9) The prophecy given to Daniel is about who? Circle one of the following.

   a. The Church   b. Israel   c. All nations

Read Daniel 10:16-21
10) Identify the person Daniel is speaking with in these verses and give your reasons for your choice.

11) What do verses eighteen and nineteen tell us about the value of God's Word?

12) How important is the war that is to take place in verses twenty and twenty-one to the Jews? Explain. See Jeremiah 30:1-3

Discussion:
How active do think demons are in our government leaders and in the world at large?

Summary Statement:
Only a believer is aware when he is in the presence of the Holy Spirit.

Accessing the Scriptures

In retrospect, Daniel records two heavenly beings who gave him visions of encouragement for Israel. In this chapter, Daniel describes where he was, <u>who he was with and how those people reacted</u>! If we read these verses carefully, it should be clear, the two heavenly beings speaking to him are Gabriel (or one like Gabriel) and Christ. For those who dispute this to be Christ, another word assures us it is Christ. Daniel addresses Him as Lord three times. Additionally, Daniel refers to himself as a servant. (v.17) Men do not serve angels! It is the other way around. Angels are servants of men. In fact, <u>man will judge angels</u>. (1 Corinthians 6:3) The reasons for this are many. Man, not angels, was created in the image of God. Second, God sends angels to serve those who inherit, His children. Third and most importantly, <u>Christ gave Himself at the Cross for the saints</u>, not angels.

Given the entire chapter is about Israel, the events in verses twenty and twenty-one are conflicts that are history for us today. Yet they happened for our benefit! Because verses twenty and twenty-one have already occurred, they seem quite small and insignificant, but this is huge! Satan did not want the Jews to return to Jerusalem and rebuild the Temple. Because out of a rebuilt Jerusalem, Christ would defeat Satan. And from a rebuilt Jerusalem, Christ's Church would emerge.

It would be Cyrus the Great who would issue the decree (Ezra 1:1-4, 2 Chronicles 36:22-23) setting in motion the <u>seventy week prophecy of Daniel</u>, which sets the stage for Revelation 6-22. This is the part where Satan and his forces are ultimately cast into the fiery furnace. (Revelation 20) If you are skeptical that demons exist, this chapter might just change your perspective.

One of Satan's more effective strategies is the delusion that the conflict between good and evil is confined to the physical world. Such delusion invites indifference and naivety, even from Christians. The war between God and Satan in the spiritual realm has not diminished, but intensified and its final battle will take place in our physical world. (Revelation 16:16)

Application

When the Holy Spirit speaks to you about a matter, be prepared to stand alone! *"For the message of the cross is foolishness to those who are perishing."* (1 Corinthians 1:18) Relative to today in matters relating to Christ, good and evil, those not living in the Spirit are uncomfortable at the Spirit's very presence. That is why unregenerate boys and girls immediately withdraw, even become hostile at the name of Jesus.

Notes for Daniel 10

DANIEL 11:1-32
Sixty-Nine Weeks of Years or 483 Years

Think of this lesson as an account of the four hundred plus years between Malachi and Matthew when God is silent. This was a period of great turmoil for Israel as wars between pagan nations raged on for centuries. As Daniel's seventy-weeks continue, God's plans, whether for nations or individuals, are unshakable. Satan has plans to detour God's plans, but his efforts will prove futile. (Revelation 20:1-3)

Read Daniel 11:1-20

1) According to verse two, what two empires will clash?

2) The mighty king in verse three and four is Alexander the Great. History records his death at the age of thirty five. What happens to his kingdom after his death?

3) a. In the conflict between Egypt to the south (v. 5) and the Assyrians to the north, what land lay between the two? View map thirteen in your Bible.

b. What do you think will result in this land in between when opposing factions collide?

Discussion:
Why do you think God allows His people to suffer at the hands of godless tyrants?

4) Compare events described in verses five through sixteen to Revelation 16:12-16.

5) a. To what nation does *"The Beautiful Land"* refer?

b. Explain God's covenant in regard to this land. Read Genesis 12:1-3

6) Using few or even one word, define covenant.

7) The first promise God made to a man, (Abraham) would be the last promise kept. Describe the fulfillment of that promise. (Revelation 21:2, 24)

8) a. Describe the character of the leader in verses seventeen through nineteen?

   b. In your lifetime, have you seen a similar world leader?

   c. Did they fall or are they still in power?

Read Daniel 11:21-32

9) Though these verses relate to a time before Christ, what does verse twenty seven and twenty nine tell you about
   a. men?

   b. God?

10) Compare verse thirty with Revelation 13:16-18

Discussion:
The Jew historically has experienced little triumph and suffered great tragedy. The nations have hated them and Anti-Semitism is widespread. In regard to God, their tragedies were self-inflected. 1) Exchange ideas why the nations hate the Jew and 2) why did God allow disaster upon disaster to Israel?

Summary Statement:
For Israel, good and bad news. A decree allows Jews to return to their homeland. Included are plans to renovate the Temple and restore the wall destroyed by the Babylonians. Sacred objects of worship would be returned and the daily sacrifice reinstituted. But a shadow is on the horizon. The ongoing struggles of men and nations to plunder and murder puts Israel directly in the path of rampaging armies.

Don't over analyze! <u>God is silent for over four hundred years</u> between Malachi and Matthew. Verses one through thirty two is an account of those silent years when the nations surrounding the Beautiful Land rage on century after century. These torrid events are God's continuing plan of Sanctification for His chosen people. Historical records detail the names and events prophesied here by Daniel. John MacArthur's Bible Commentary 'Unleashing God's Truth, One Verse at a Time' is an excellent source if you are inclined to do some extra reading.

At verse thirty three, (next lesson) jump ahead 2500 years and we get a vision of the same rage of nations but this time, <u>compressed into two, forty-two month segments</u>. You say, how can we jump ahead 2500 years? After the Diaspora following the time of Christ and the Roman destruction of Jerusalem in 70 A.D., there is nothing to write about concerning Israel.

In God's Mercy, the Gentile is grafted into God's plan. (Romans 11:17-24) <u>The Church Age is like a sporting event timeout</u>. This study takes the position a timeout occurs between verses thirty two and thirty three. (2500 yrs. and counting) Therefore, up to verse thirty two for us is history! Our finite mind will resist jumping ahead 2500 years but remember this; *"with the Lord a day is like a thousand years."* (2 Peter 3:8, Psalm 90:4) Verse thirty six, *"the time of wrath"* is Daniel's seventieth week which supports this being a future time. This is further supported by Jeremiah 30:7 *"the time of Jacob's trouble"* and *"after this."* (Revelation 4:1) The Church Age is a time out in God's plan for Israel. Sixty-nine weeks are history with only the seventieth week remaining.

Mede-Persia defeated Babylon. Three Persian kings are followed by a fourth, more powerful king (Xerxes 1) who would come against Greece. He is defeated by Alexander the Great whose empire quickly expanded. But his life was cut short and his kingdom split into four parts. The Ptolemies controlled the southern part including Egypt. The Seleucids held the north. (Syria/Babylonia) The struggle was for the control of Palestine. A militant sect of Judaism (Maccabees) came against the Seleucids with some success. (v. 31) A northern leader, *Antiochus Epiphanes set out to exterminate the Jews. During his reign, the altar at Jerusalem was desecrated. *"The abomination that brings desolation."* (v. 31) *"The invader will do as he pleases; no one will be able to stand against him. He will establish himself in the Beautiful Land and will have the power to destroy it."* (v. 16)

Antiochus Epiphanes fades from view as the Roman Empire emerges, but his horrendous acts in Jerusalem remain to this day, <u>foretelling of antichrist</u>.

* Like Roman Caesar's, there were as many as 4 Seleucid kings named Antiochus. It is not the purpose of this study to identify each by number.

<u>Application</u>

Diminishing the character of a Christian is Satan's greatest weapon against Christ! Satan need not physically kill the membership of your Church. He can be just as effective by killing the spiritual effectiveness of its individual members.

Notes for Daniel 11:1-32

DANIEL 11:33 – DANIEL 12:13
Daniel's Seventieth Week

Antichrist's brief, but violent rise and fall! God doesn't reveal to Daniel a specific date for the time of the end, but He does reveal how it will end.

Read Daniel 11:33-45

1) If you were to choose one verse that reveals the character of antichrist, which verse would you choose? Explain your reason.

2) In your own words, describe *"the time of wrath."* [Read Revelation 19:11-21]

Discussion:

If indeed the time described here is the seventieth week, Daniel is describing events of the seven year Tribulation. Revelation six through nineteen unfolds the details. The very mention of Edom, Moab, Ammon and Egypt suggests that the invader from the north is not Arab, but either Mongolians from China or European (Roman/Russian). Many believe the invading armies from the north to be led by Russia. Verse forty one indicates whoever the invaders may be, they will have trouble in the Arab world. How do you think the western world, the Americas, Canada and Mexico fit in?

Read Daniel 12:1-4

3) a. What people will the angel Michael be protecting during the seven year Tribulation? [See Revelation 7:1-8]

   b. Noticeably missing in these apocalyptic events is the Church! Why is the Church missing? See 1 Corinthians 15:52, 1 Thessalonians 4:16

4) Verse 12:1 speaks of names entered into a book. What Book is being referred to? See Revelation 20:12

5) What are Daniel's final instructions? (v. 4)

Discussion of Daniel 12:5-7

In addition to the man in linen, (Christ) two other men appear. It is not as important to identify who the two men are as much as it is to give thought to the significance if any, that the two men are on opposite sides of the river. What might opposite sides of the river suggest if anything?

Read Daniel 12:8-13

6) What is Daniel's response to the conversations of the three beings? (v. 8)

7) a. Until Christ returns, what good things will occur? (v. 10)

   b. What bad things will continue? (v. 10)

8) What does Christ relate to Daniel on a personal level he can expect?

9) Physical death is not the same as spiritual death. What does the New Testament reveal happens to the Spirit of a believer upon physical death? See Philippians 1:23

Discussion:

[See Luke 23:39-43] One thief was saved that day. What does Jesus' words to him reveal in regard to the man's soul? What also does this say about water baptism or lack thereof in this man's case?

10) Name two or more things you come away with after having studied Daniel?

Summary Statement:

What Daniel seals, Christ unseals! See Revelation 6:1

This chapter, like all of Daniel, has to do with the Jewish people but it still remains, Jew and Gentile alike will ultimately be caught up both in crisis and in victory. Like the previous chapter, the readings here are directly related to Chapter 10 with Daniel describing his experience with heavenly beings.

It should be noted there are those who hold to the concept that antichrist is not a person, but rather a concept or world system. This position might be supported by 1 John 4:3 but it doesn't account for 1 Thessalonians 2:3-4 which distinctly identifies antichrist as an individual. This study holds to the position antichrist is as much a real person as was Antiochous Epiphanes. Many speculate as to his identity. Political figures often are tagged with being him by their opponents. *Daniel 11:37 is the Bible's best verse to identify who he will be for those interested in knowing.

(* Note: It is advisable to compare this verse with different bibles, including the amplified bible.)

Final Observation

An additional study of Ezra and Nehemiah is required if one wishes to detail portions of Daniel's prophecy concerning Jewish history after their return from exile. Many Jews chose to remain in Babylon. They had followed the words of the prophet Jeremiah (Jeremiah 29:5) to build a normal life in Babylon. The younger set, having blended in with Babylonian society, didn't necessarily return to Jerusalem. They most likely are the ones spared the persecutions that would take place there.

If at times, you found the readings difficult, who among us engaged in a conversation with our Lord could even write our name, much less write the extraordinary accounts Daniel received. Daniel was not chosen based on his writing gifts, he was chosen because he was highly esteemed of God. <u>So let us not argue the details, but simply thrill at what has been revealed</u>. Perhaps God purposely veils His plans to test you and me in whatever He wishes to test us. In the final analysis, Christians need not agree on details but rather, marvel at the reliability of the Word of God! Maranatha!

Application

For the believer, Daniel's account of the authority of God offers enormous comfort to this truth, <u>God' sovereignty will never be superseded by the might of fallible men.</u> Or will His authority be compromised by the cunning schemes of the devil! Christian, armed with this assurance, how ought you to be living?

Notes for Daniel 11:33 – 12:13

Twenty One Lessons The Book of

Revelation

ANTICHRIST, WAR, FAMINE, DEATH

VICTORIOUS CHRIST

CONGRATULATIONS

You are embarking on a part of the Bible many avoid or perhaps study for the wrong reason. If you have participated in an earlier study of Revelation, be prepared not only to affirm things learned from your earlier study, be prepared to discover new truths. Guard against being too rigid to change your mind should the Word lead you to do so.

It is vital to know what this book is about. It is first about Jesus Christ, His position and the reliability of God's Prophetic Word concerning Jesus throughout the Bible. After Christ, this book is about Israel. This study wishes to make clear that yes, the spirit of antichrist will persecute the Church from its inception, but we wish to make clear that the coming Wrath is not against the Church or will the Church be present in the *"time of Jacob's trouble".* Trying to infuse the Church into the Tribulation is to disregard Jeramiah, Daniel's seventieth week and 1 Thessalonians 4:13-18. It will be Israel and an unrepentant earth that experience the Great Tribulation! Did not God remove both Noah and Lott prior to raining down destruction? The Bride of Christ shall not experience the Wrath of God. As Noah, his family, Lot and his people were spared, so shall God's Church be spared. To this end, Christ gave Himself up for Her. <u>What groom brings wrath upon His bride</u>? Whatever persecution comes upon the Church, it will not come from above! Jesus' Olivet discourse was solely about Israel. Revelation 6-19 will be upon Israel and unrepentant men who are left behind.

John's Imax Panorama of Daniel's Seventieth Week and Beyond into Eternity

Picture if you will, John seated in a theater with seven screens before him all playing at the same time and behind him is an eighth screen which doesn't come to life until the other seven screens finish their story. <u>Chapter two and three are God's evaluation of His Church and not a part of John's vision of Daniel's seventieth week.</u>

Main Theme

1,4,5,6,8,9,10,14,15,16,19

144 Thousand	**2 Witnesses**
7	11
Woman & Dragon	**2 Beasts**
12	13
Woman on a Beast	**Other Events**
17-18	Scattered

JOHN

1000 Years and Beyond

20, 21, 22

INTRODUCTION TO REVELATION

Why study prophecy? Will I be a better person? Will it change anything? What does prophecy have to do with faith and love? The answer lies at the conclusion of this study! *"Blessed is the one who reads the words of this prophecy, and blessed are those who hear it and take to heart what is written in it, because the time is near."* (Revelation 1:3)

The title is singular, Revelation! Please be correct when speaking this word. Christ is the Revelation! He is positioned at Heaven's Throne. The earth is about to become His footstool. From heaven, He will descend back to earth as King of Kings and Lord of Lords. Jesus Christ is the focus of this final book of the Bible. This truth is revealed in Chapter one! What follows are intricate programs only a great God could orchestrate. There is a program for Daniel's seventieth week for Israel, programs for the saints of God, the Church, for unregenerate men, for the apostate church, for Satan and his crowd and the Millennial Kingdom.

Daniel was God's choice to receive and record numerous visions because he was highly esteemed of God. (Daniel 10:11) So John too, was highly esteemed. (John 20:2) John was a fisherman with his brother James when Jesus called them to be Disciples. (Matthew 4:21-22) Little did John know the plans God had for him. John receives God's Revelation while he is imprisoned on the Island of Patmos off the coast of Turkey.

John was witness to incredible events during Jesus' Ministry. He was present when <u>Jesus was Glorified.</u> (John 12:16, 23, 28-30) He was present when <u>Jesus was Transfigured.</u> (Matthew 17:1-8, Mark 9:2-8, Luke 9:28-36) He was present at the <u>Ascension of Jesus.</u> (Mark 16:19-20, Luke 24:36-51, Acts 1:6-1) He accompanied Jesus during <u>countless miracles</u> and teachings. Years pass and now John is granted a look into heaven and glory. He sees Christ as He is, Mighty God!

In this study you are going to encounter heaven and hell. If you have errant concepts of their location, even their existence, you will be challenged to exchange myth and people's opinions for biblical truth. You will see gentle Jesus in a new role. <u>For those who don't want to know Jesus as anything but the Lamb of God, loving and kind, you would not only be naïve, you would be unbiblical.</u> Yes, God is Love, but God also is Just! *"He is King of Kings and Lord of Lords!"* (Revelation 19:16) People who are so focused on faith and love and perceive this book as neither, will find this final book of the Holy Scriptures is the culmination of both.

Whether you have studied this remarkable section of the Bible or this is your first venture, resolve not to bring <u>baseless preconceived ideas</u> to this study. <u>Allow the Scriptures to speak to you</u>. For only in them is Truth to be found. According to His Promise, the just and unjust will receive what is due them.

REVELATION 1
Hope for Tomorrow

Because of where Jesus is today, you have a hope for tomorrow! If you love the Lord Jesus, this chapter is for you! If you haven't accepted Jesus as your Lord and Savior, this chapter is for you too! It is time you do! This book is the Bible's final warning to unregenerate men and women! Every sin committed will either be pardoned at the cross or paid for in hell!

Discussion Questions
Who will win the next presidential election? Super bowl? World Series?
Why do you think people are so fascinated with the future?

What are some useless things people do to reveal the future?
Have you ever consulted a palm reader or tarot card reader for counsel?

What does the Bible say about fortune telling? See Deuteronomy 18:10-12
Fortune telling seems so harmless. Why is God so opposed to this activity?

Read Revelation 1:1-6
1) Jesus is who He said He was! What does that mean to you?

2) You have family and friends who are lost. What can you do for them?

3) Grace (v. 4) is a Christian greeting referring to the cross and peace was a three-fold Jewish greeting referring to peace with self, others and God. John's use of both words in his greetings suggests what?

4) Which two verses identify the Trinity of God?

5) The number seven implies perfection. Using Acts 1:5, 8 and Isaiah 11:2, identify the sevenfold work of the Holy Spirit.

Discussion:
What does it mean to be a Priest of God? (v.6) [See 1 Peter 2:9]

Read Revelation 1:7-11
6) At Christ's return even those who pierced Him will see Him. But those people have been dead for centuries, so who living today has pierced Him?

Discussion:

If God's people will be joyful to see Him, explain *"all the peoples of the earth will mourn because of Him."* If your theology of 1 Thessalonians 4:17 and similar Scripture is flawed, you have a dilemma inhibiting a correct understanding of the seventieth week of Daniel for which much of Revelation is about.

Time out: It is not the purpose of this study to debate the Rapture. This study takes the position that 1 Thessalonians 4:17 settles the debate. A body of people are going to be removed prior to the seventieth week of Daniel and that group is the Church.

7) What is the significance of how John identifies himself in verse nine?

Read Revelation 1:12-20

8) Using the glossary for this chapter, explain Christ's relationship with His Church.

9) With the aid of the glossary for this chapter, how would you describe Christ in more understandable words that a friend would understand?

10) a. Describe the reaction of John. (v. 17)

     b. Describe the action of Jesus. (v. 17)

11) What does Jesus say about Himself? (v. 18)

12) What is it God has commissioned John to do?

Discussion:

From drawings and photographs you have seen of Jesus, how might this chapter challenge your view of Him?

Summary Statement:

John relates to believers of all generations that Christ is where He said He was going in the Gospel of John and is preparing to hold court beginning with the Church.

 **Leader's Helicopter Overview for Revelation 1**

(Optional or Prepare Your Own)

The Gospels are but a part of the story. The Book of Revelation is the rest of the story. John had witnessed much with an earthly Jesus. He knew the humiliation of his Master's Crucifixion as a common thief. Certainly John knew Jesus as God Incarnate but still, John was so overcome at the actual sight of Jesus as God that he immediately fell to his knees (v. 17). *"We have known Christ in the flesh, henceforth we will know Him no more."* (2 Corinthians 5:16) Those who reject the Trinity because the actual word does not appear in the Bible need to read verses four and five. These two verses testify to a Triune God. Lampstand is a direct reference to the Church and prepares us for the next two chapters. Before Christ Judges unregenerate men and the world system, He will first Judge His Church. (2 Corinthians 5:10)

No chapter in the Bible is like this chapter. Earthly Jesus is God. He is Creator of all there is! The believer is assured what has been told throughout the New Testament is true. For the unbeliever, Revelation is a call to repentance! (Luke 13:1-5)

Don't be alarmed by the abundant use of imagery. A glossary is available to assist you. Imagery is not weakened by time and would puzzle the Romans should they bring charges against Christians for defying Domitian's orders to worship him. Symbols can represent value systems; i.e. Babylon conveys spiritual corruption. Harlot conveys worship infidelity. The people of John's generation were familiar with Old Testament symbolism so their appearance in John's letter would not be as problematic as in our generation. To interpret a term apart from how it appeared in the Old Testament is to misinterpret it.

Going forward, you will not see Jesus as the gentle Jewish carpenter as our hymns portray Him. What you will see, is a Victorious King. Do not be too concerned with minute details. Rather, it is this book's timeless truths you want to take with you.

Oh for a thousand tongues to sing, my great Redeemer's praise
The glories of my God and King, the triumphs of His grace.
My gracious Master and My God, assist me to proclaim.
To spread through all the earth abroad, the honors of Thy Name.
He breaks the power of canceled sin, He sets the prisoner free.
His blood can make the foulest clean, His blood availed for me.
Words of John Wesley

Application

Because of where Jesus is today, you have a hope for tomorrow! Rest well my Christian friend, John confirms by sight what you and I accept by faith. All things Jesus said of Himself are true! Maranatha!

Glossary of Imagery by Verse for Revelation 1

v. 4	seven spirits	sevenfold ministry of the Holy Spirit (Isaiah 11:2)
v. 6	priests	believers may enter God's presence (Hebrews 5:1-10)
v. 7	clouds	supernatural clouds of glory, not CO2 clouds
v. 7	mourn	not about repentance - about anticipation of Judgment
v. 10	trumpet	like a trumpet, (penetrating) not a literal trumpet
v. 12	lampstands	seven churches - symbolic of all churches, then and now
v. 14	flame of fire	fire represents Judgment (Revelation 19:12)
v. 15	feet-bronze	Christ is moving through His people (Church)
v. 15	bronze	was a part of the Altar of His people (Exodus 18:1-7)
v. 15	many waters	convergence - culmination force like that of Niagara Falls
v. 16	seven stars	Pastors - Church leadership
v. 16	hand	Christ controls His Church
v. 16	two edged sword	cuts deep-cuts two ways - believers and unbelievers
v. 17	first and last	Yahweh was before any god and will be the One final God
v. 18	hold the keys	Christ will judge the world (Acts 17:31)
v. 18	death and Hades	death is a state of being - Hades has an address
v. 20	angels	messengers of God - usually a heavenly being but here it is people same as seven stars which are Church leaders.......

Notes for Revelation 1

Accessing the Scriptures

REVELATION 2
Christ Evaluates His Church

Scripture is timeless and human nature is today what human nature was 2000 years ago. Therefore, Scripture remains relevant throughout all generations. Christ's evaluation of the strengths and weaknesses of first century Christians gives us insight into our own condition today. Consider your own strengths and weaknesses as you study these next two chapters.

Read Revelation 2:1-7

1) What does it mean to be led by the power of the Holy Spirit? See Isaiah 11:2

2) First Read 2 Timothy 3:1-5 and James 2:22. The people of the Ephesian Church had successfully identified individuals who claimed to be Christian but their actions told a much different story. How are such individuals destructive to the faith?

3) What does it mean to put Christ first? See Deuteronomy 6:5, Mark 12:30

Read Revelation 2:8-11

4) Unless you live outside the United States, persecution as described in these verses is less severe but is not absent.

   a. How do you see people of faith targeted in today's society?

   b. Have family, friends or the workplace discriminated against you because you are a Christian?

   c. How much do you compromise your faith just to fit in or advance?

5) [Read Romans 9:6-7] Are there individuals you view as religious, who go to church, attend Bible study, yet quite possibly are not saved? Why?

Read Revelation 2:12-25

6) a. What is the mission of the Church? See Matthew 28:16-20, Acts 1:8

   b. What are some things that can compromise the effectiveness of the Church?

   c. What things do you do that bring discredit to the faith?

7) Within the home and within the Church, what damage can be done by wrongful teaching in regard to the way of Salvation?

8) In your experience, have you ever been exposed to errant teachings either by parents or the Church? How does legalism displace Grace?

"The words of the wise are more to be heeded than the shouts of a ruler of fools."

Ecclesiastes 9:17

Discussion:

Do you believe this statement? "The apostate church sends more people to hell than the opinions of a thousand Atheists." How dangerous are Cults to the souls of people? Which do you think is worse, unbelief or errant belief? Why?

Read Revelation 2:26-29

9) a. What authority will believers have in the Kingdom of Christ? (v. 26)
      See 1 Corinthians 6:2-3, Psalm 2:8-9

   b. When will that authority take place? See Revelation 20:4-6

Summary Statement:

The four Churches represented in this chapter reveal not much has changed in two thousand years! Christians in parts of the world still suffer atrocities and false teachers are everywhere.

What a wonderful chapter to get a look into the mind of God and how He evaluates His Church. This chapter and the following chapter are unique in that, <u>God is looking at His Church and nothing else</u>! Immediately jumping off the pages is that nothing is out of God's sight! Christ, having suffered and died for the Church, <u>abhors being in second place</u>! Second place is manifest when a Church body places a higher value on programs over worship and devotion. One of the great dangers to spiritual decay is the Church with a panacea for elaborate campuses, programs out the kazoo, private planes etc... With miss-directed emphasis, devotion sits at the back of the auditorium. This may seem harsh but is it?

Does this mean small churches are spiritually stronger than large churches? <u>It means look before you establish a Church home</u>! How people choose the church they attend is often based on errant criteria; the preacher is a great orator, the building is impressive, it is a short drive, all my friends go there, they have wonderful youth programs, the music is terrific. Every one of these reasons are the wrong reasons to select a Church. <u>Satan is also in the church business</u> and we know he is a liar and a deceiver. *"For your enemy the devil prowls around like a roaring lion seeking someone to devour."* (2 Peter 5:8) <u>This passage is not talking about external enemies</u>. This passage is about the internal, one's own heart and the Church community. It is about being alert to false teaching, worldliness and watered down devotion.

If you expose yourself long enough to false doctrines you are in danger of replacing truth with lies. <u>Grace gets replaced by works or a combination of the two</u>. This occurs within the walls of religious institutions, large or small that burden its members with a laundry list of do's and don'ts or mandated rituals. They are like the Swedish ship Vesa. This ship displayed elaborate ornamentation that included sixty-eight canons. The outside looked great but a grave error lay hidden within! In 1628 this ornate ship set sail from Stockholm for its maiden voyage. <u>Overloaded with man-made objects</u>, the ship promptly sank less than a mile out, taking fifty-three seamen to their death.

Then there are the churches who say if you are not a member of their sect or denomination you are lost. Nonsense, such an attitude is little more than obstinate religious aristocracy.

<u>Application</u>

Christ loved the Church! He gave Himself for Her! Don't select a church that waters this down, either with false teaching, secular commercialism or religious aristocracy.

Glossary of Imagery by Verse for Revelation 2

v. 4	first love	Christ in first place - not religious rituals or legalism
v. 6	Nicolaitans	apostates who pervert Grace as being a license to sin
v. 7	tree of life	true believer's assurance of Eternal Life
v. 11	overcomes	identity of a saved man or woman
v. 11	second death	the first death is physical-the second death is eternal (Revelation 20:6)
v. 14	Balaam	a false doctrine defined today as apostasy
v. 17	hidden manna	Eternal Life hidden from skeptics but revealed to believers
v. 17	white stone	winning athlete's invitation to attend the victory celebration
v. 17	new name	a private new name for believers (See Isaiah 62:2)

Note: Angels, stars, lampstands represent pastors, leaders, Churches.

Notes for Revelation 2

REVELATION 3
Church Evaluation Continued

Worldliness is a deadly affliction because it focuses on a life style that lives for the pleasures of now. Worldliness is counter to Jesus' words in the Sermon on the Mount: *"Do not store up for your selves treasures on earth where moth and rust destroy, where thieves break in and steal. But store up for yourselves treasures in heaven. Where your treasure is, there also is your heart."* (Paraphrased from Matthew 6:19-21)

Read Revelation 3:1-6

1) What would you say are some problems with a Church whose doctrine is correct, whose teachings are true, yet spiritually they are dead?

2) How might a Church be compared to a country club?

Discussion:

Is it fair to make judgments on a Church? Why or why not?

3) Cite examples how Christ might be used as a commodity.

4) How serious do you think indifference is to a marriage relationship?

5) Where love once was in a relationship, what changes take place that might lead to humdrum routine and loss of passion for the relationship?

Discussion:

Discuss how complacency might be manifested in a Church and what might be done to avoid this destructive malaise?

6) Life is a series of hills and valleys. In a believer's relationship with the Lord, do you think valleys will occur in one's faith? Do you believe once saved, always saved? Do you know your Bible well enough to support this?

7) Standing water stagnates and the same is true spiritually. What are some ways to keep one's faith alive and active? See 1 Peter 2:1-2

8) Since your conversion, how is your progress as in 1 Peter 2:1-2?

Read Revelation 3:7-22

9) Explain the promise of verse nine. See Psalm 2:8-9, Revelation 20:2, 6

10) What is it that you find quite different with the Church at Philadelphia and Smyrna from the other five Churches?

11) What positives, if any do you find in the Church at Laodicea?

Time out: Some Eschatologists suggest that the Seven Churches represent Church progression and that we are in the time of the Church at Philadelphia. They further suggest at the conclusion of the Philadelphian period, the Church will be taken up, leaving only a Church such as the one at Laodicea. Possible, but don't be misled, Scripture does speak of <u>Tribulation Saints. People saved after removal of the Church</u>. Perhaps it is those who refuse the mark of 666.

Discussion:
What are your thoughts about the Church's greatest successes in today's modern world? What are its greatest failures?

Summary Statement:
There is a paradox in the Church. It is the uncomfortable situation between what the Church claims to be and what it comes across as being.

Optional:
Draft a brief evaluation letter you think Christ would send to you. (Sharing is optional) Which of the Seven Churches best describes a Church you have attended?

 **Leader's Helicopter Overview for Revelation 3**
(Optional or Prepare Your Own)

In a review of the first verse of each of the seven letters, Christ establishes His authority to sit in Judgment of His Church and the individual members.

Of this chapter, only Philadelphia receives honor. Issues exists at the other two churches but interestingly, false doctrine and teachings are not among them. These two things not being the problem, let us consider other criteria how Christ looks at a Church and its people. Early in His Earthly Ministry, Jesus taught the principles of Kingdom life. His Sermon on the Mount (Matthew 5, 6 and 7) began with the Beatitudes. In them, He describes the Christian Life. Arguably, the summary statement for this early teaching is Matthew 6:20-21; *"store up for yourselves treasures in heaven, where moths and vermin do not destroy and where thieves do no break in and steal. For where your treasure is, there your heart will be also."* When Christian living is incorporated in a Church, we get the results described at Philadelphia and Smyrna.

If a church today doesn't resemble the one at Philadelphia, these folks must be attending church for the wrong reason! Let's explore some possibilities that contribute to spiritual failure. Perhaps they only come to church simply to use it! It is a safe place to engage their kids in activities – it is an opportunity to sing or play an instrument – it is a lucrative venue to make business contacts – it will enhance one's political career. In essence, the Church becomes a religious country club, a conduit to meet a secular need. The people at Sardis and Laodicea claimed to know Christ but they did not belong to Him. [See Matthew 7:21-23, 2 Timothy 3:5]

One disturbing trend today are politicians who appear to use Christ as a commodity to gain advantage in a targeted political base rather than reach the lost. Surely they don't realize the grave danger they are in. Just ask the folks at the Laodicean Church.

Ah yes, Laodicea, the Church of hypocrites, pretenders if you will! Of the Seven Churches, this one is void of even one true Christian! If the Rapture occurred, their attendance Sunday morning would remain unchanged! The Church would be full. The musicians, teachers, ushers, deacons, even the pastors would all be present. Yes, all profess Christ, but born again they were not! Church is only for appearances!

Application

From burdensome doctrine, to false teaching to Christian living, let us continually examine the Word so that we fully understand John 15:7-8.

"If you abide in Me, and My words abide in you, you will ask what you desire, and it shall be done for you. By this My Father is glorified, that you bear much fruit; so you will be my disciples"
John 15:7-8 (NKJV)

Glossary of Imagery by Verse for Revelation 3

v. 1	alive, but dead	large congregation - few saved
v. 3	come as a thief	refers to 1 Thessalonians 4:17 (caught up)
v. 5	overcomes	those regenerated through Christ
v. 5	book of life	promise of eternal life (Revelation 20:12)
v. 7	Philadelphia	city named after a king who loved his brother
v. 7	key of David	Christ's authority as to who enters His Kingdom (Revelation 1:18)
v. 10	hour of trial	forty-two months of the most extreme persecution (Revelation 13:5)
v. 11	coming quickly	at the start of Daniel's seventieth week (Daniel 9:24-27) Christ will quickly remove the Church from the coming Wrath - caught up (1 Thessalonians 4:17)
v. 11	pillar-my God	identified as belonging to God
v. 12	New Jerusalem	the capitol city of the Coming Kingdom
v. 14	faithful true witness	Christ
v. 14	ruler of creation	Jesus was in the beginning God - not later created
v. 16	lukewarm	refers to Laodicea's foul tasting Sulfur water
v. 16	vomit you out	self-deceived hypocrites sickens Christ
v. 18	refined gold	godly works as opposed to hypocritical works
v. 19	love-rebuke-discipline	Christ loves His Church, but this one needs to repent
v. 20	knock at the door	found lacking - Christ asks to enter this Church - challenges even one member to answer His call to genuine faith

Notes for Revelation 3

Accessing the Scriptures

REVELATION 4
Adoration

This chapter is pivotal! Since The Book of Acts, the New Testament has been about the Church, its responsibilities of winning souls and walking in righteousness. This chapter looks now at Kingdom life. We immediately see Kingdom life <u>begins with Worship</u>.

O' come, let us adore Him, O' come, let us adore Him,
O' come, let us adore Him, Christ the Lord.

Read Revelation 4:1-11

1) Certainly God is glorified by righteous living but might there be more?

    a. List ways other than righteous living Christians engage worship.

    b. On a scale from one to ten, how would you rank your worship? _____

2) Compare John's experience with the prophet Ezekiel. See Ezekiel 1:1, 11:24

3) What similar things did John see that Ezekiel also saw? See Ezekiel 1:5-10

4) Compare John's experience with the Apostle Paul. See 2 Corinthians 1-4

5) Of what significance is the image of a rainbow? See Genesis 9:12-17

6) This chapter inspired the hymn "Holy, Holy, Holy." Using a hymnal, name three hymns that were inspired from Scripture.
    a.

    b.

    c.

7) From memory, write the first verse of "Amazing Grace"

Time out: if you don't know the Lord Jesus isn't it time you do? Time is running out and one day it will be too late! Right where you sit, say these words; Jesus, I know your name but I don't know you. Help me to dedicate my life to you. What you did for me I can never repay except to give myself to you. Come into my life. I confess you as my Lord and Savior this very moment. I humbly accept your offer of forgiving grace. Receive me into Thy good grace. Amen.

8) How important do you think hymn singing is?

9) Sadly, when congregations stand to sing a hymn, many simply just stand there like a bump on a log doing nothing but occupying space. How true is this statement? Worship is not a spectator sport!

10) Do you think heaven will be a place where one can opt out of worship?

11) Your glossary suggests the twenty-four living elders are the Church. How does the dress of the twenty-four elders and the crowns on their heads help to identify this is so? See Revelation 3:4-5, Isaiah 35:10

12) John paints a word picture of God in His heaven. From John's description, describe heaven in your words.

13) In chapters two and three Christ evaluates the condition of the Church. This chapter and chapter one are similar in that, both are descriptive.

   a. How are chapters 1 and 4 similar?

   b. How are chapters 1 and 4 different?

Summary Statement:
The four living creatures illustrate that God's glory extends well beyond the Church and its mission. This chapter calls for you and I to recognize the Infinity of God. In doing this, our response is to instinctively worship Him.

"After this" appears twice in the first verse. When God repeats Himself, He intends to make a point! If we miss His point here, chances are we will not understand the next sixteen chapters correctly. After what? - The Church age! Since the Book of Acts, the Church has been the Bible's focus of the Gospel message. Going forward, the Church is noticeably absent because it is no longer here! (1 Thessalonians 4:17) Oh, there will a facsimile of a Church, but it is the apostate church, the Great Prostitute! But its end is near as you will discover. (Revelation 17-18)

Time out: We can't go any farther and do so accurately until the subject of the removal of the true Church is resolved. The next sixteen chapters are an unfolding of God's wrath on unregenerate people. God haters if you will. Shall the Bride of Christ suffer the same wrath prepared for those who reject the Grace of God? *"It is written, eye has not seen, or ear heard, nor have entered into the heart of man the things which God has prepared for those who love Him."* (1 Corinthians 2:9) Certainly God's people endure trials but what is coming is world ending wrath, not trials!

If we do not accept the removal of the Church at verse one, the next sixteen chapters would coalesce the Church with Israel and Daniel Ten, Eleven and Twelve would make no sense. No, the program for the Church ends with verse one. The next sixteen chapters are God's program for Israel. This is alluded to in Daniel's seventieth week.

Yes, the Church is gone to heaven! But we will see Her again in a different form. In chapter nineteen She reappears as the Bride of Christ. What a glorious event that will be! Your focus on things of this life will be no more. Instead you, like any bride, only see the future before you. A future with Christ Jesus at your side. A life without heartache. Maranatha!

Of this chapter Warren Wiersbe concludes, Christians do not balance witnessing and working for Christ with worship of Him. Wiersbe subscribes that <u>heaven is place of worship</u> and God's people will Worship Him throughout eternity. Certainly it would seem, if our worship equals our work output, our prayer life can't help but improve.

Application

<u>Worship can neither be a spectator sport or a casual option</u>. We instinctively must engage worship at every opportunity, be it singing, praising or in prayer. It is in these things we can be comfortably prepared to engage and take part in heaven! *"I come as a thief in the night."* Thief ascribes to the suddenness Christ will take His true Church to heaven just prior to Daniel's seventieth week. Open a hymnal and practice.

Glossary of Imagery by Verse for Revelation 4

v. 1	after this	refers to the Church Age
v. 2	in the Spirit	not a dream - it is as if John had died
v. 2	throne	when used is always a place (never an object) of Divine Authority
v. 3	rainbow	God's Covenant with all living creatures - never again will He use flood waters to vent His Wrath (Genesis 9:12-17)
v. 4	twenty four elders	identity debated - Israel is not yet redeemed so it can't represent Twelve Tribes of Israel - can't represent the Twelve Apostles because some are still living including John - Tribulation saints are not yet martyred. By the process of elimination only the Church is redeemed.
v. 5	lightning	not an earthly storm - the fury of an angry God brewing
v. 5	Seven Spirits	the Holy Spirit - Seven represents perfection (Zechariah 4:2-6)
v. 6	sea of glass	clear as crystal allows light beams to radiate with glorious purity
v. 6	four creatures	identity debated - some say represents man – animals - wild beast -birds of the air - Ezekiel 1 suggests the total Awesomeness of God
v. 6	full of eyes	God's power to be all knowing - all seeing
v. 7	lion	God's strength and power
v. 7	calf	the humility and tenderness of Jesus
v. 7	man	rational intelligent being - only one created in the Image of God
v. 10	crowns	man's crowns are not equal to the crown of the King of Kings

Notes for Revelation 4

REVELATION 5
Worthy Is the Lamb

This chapter is a continuum of chapter four. The scene remains heaven. It appears the glorified Church is present. (vv. 4, 8, 11) (1 Corinthians 6:2-3) Jesus established His worthiness by never allowing sin into his life. (Matthew 3:17, 5:17) (2 Corinthians. 5:21) Jesus' oneness with the Father established His Deity. (John 10:27-30) The Psalmist writes that one day the earth shall be His Kingdom. (Psalm 2:7-9) It is fitting this chapter ends with a worship service.

Read Revelation 5:1-6

1) Having created the earth, God established Himself as landlord over it. To whom did He give dominion over the earth? See Genesis 1:26-27, 2:22

2) A landlord expects tenants to abide by his rules. If they don't, warnings are issued! What happens when tenants ignore a landlord's warnings?

3) Men and women were to tend to the earth under God's authority but whose authority did they choose to follow? See Genesis 3:1-7

4) Compare Revelation 6:15-17 with Genesis 3:8-10

5) The scroll as it is unrolled reveals among other things, God's plan to evict all who rebel against His authority. Rebellious people will be judged even unto their death!

   a. Explain John's emotion. (v. 4)

   b. Who is qualified to pronounce Judgment on others?

Discussion:

The scroll about to be opened is the same scroll that was sealed in Daniel 12:4, 9. From Daniel 12:1-4 do you think the scroll is about Judgment, about title to earth, about Israel, or all of the above?

Time out: We who are Gentles are prone to see Christ in light of the Church and little else. Let us not forget, God made numerous covenants with only Jews such as Abraham and David that have not yet been fulfilled. The Church needs to be reminded of this verse; *"I was sent only to the lost sheep of Israel."* (Matthew 15:24) We who are Gentiles are truly fortunate that a Merciful God has shed His Grace upon us also. Jesus spoke of God's inclusive Grace in Matthew 15:28.

Scriptures relating to Israel far exceeds scriptures relating to the Church. In fact, the Church is not mentioned in the Old Testament. If we consider an athletic event, the Church is only relevant during one timeout. [Church Age]

> *"How great is the love, the Father has lavished on us,*
> *that we should be called children of God"*
> (1 John 3:1)

6) a. Who is the Lion of Judah that is from the linage of David?

   b. Who is the Lamb of God?

   c. How would you explain One Person being identified with such contrasting animal images?

Read Revelation 5:7-14

7) The new song (v. 9-10) (See glossary) is a hymn that anticipates the coming Kingdom when Christ will reign with His saints one thousand years. (Revelation 20:1-6) Describe the activities and location you think verse ten represents.

8) Who are the various beings John sees gathered at this worship service?

Summary Statement:

In a continuation from chapter four, John is witnessing the totality of Christ! Having fulfilled the law, Jesus was worthy to be the Sacrificial Lamb and a Righteous Judge. His victory over death established His Sovereign power. He was a Son worthy to inherit the earth.

Christ has promised a Kingdom for His people and before He gives it to them, He is going to clean it up. God doesn't give corrupted gifts!

A scroll is our subject. John observes the scroll has writings on both sides which is significant! If this is the same scroll from Daniel 12:4 and surely it is, since the time of the Babylonian exile, space on the scroll was maxed out. There is no room to add anything. What you are about to read and study was written and sealed five hundred years before Christ! That is pretty wild! What Daniel sealed circa 500 B.C., Christ will unseal centuries later!

The twenty-five hundred plus years between Daniel sealing the scroll and Christ unsealing it, *"the time of the Gentiles"* occurs. This period began when Cyrus the Great signed a proclamation allowing Jews to return to Jerusalem from their exile in Babylon. They would restore the city, rebuild the walls and reestablish the Temple. Daniel and Jeremiah are good sources for insight on Jewish history. If this twenty-five hundred years were an athletic event, it would be a very long time out. We should not confuse *"the time of the Gentiles"* and the Church age. They end the same time but their start time was four hundred years apart. One represents Zion being under Gentile domination, the other represents the cross and events that follow.

How long this twenty-five hundred year timeout lasts is a subject on which many books are sold. Do not be misled by those who predict the Second Coming. Even when the Church is taken out the Second Coming is still seven years away. These are two separate events separated by the Tribulation years. Not everyone will see Christ when the Church is taken up. Only His sheep will hear His voice and be received unto Him (John 10:14-16) It is not until Christ returns in final victory will every eye see Him. (Philippians 2:10)

"I do not want you to be ignorant of this mystery brothers, so that you may not be conceited: Israel has experienced a hardening in part until the full number of the Gentiles has come in. And so all Israel will be saved." (Romans 11:25-26) *"After this,"* is back to Israel and Daniel's seventieth week ticks down earth's final seven years.

Application

Why should the Judgments be of interest to the Church if it is not a part of it? <u>To understand the totality of the Holiness of God</u>!

Christians need never doubt their faith. John witnessed the risen Christ (Chapter 1) at the Throne of heaven! (Chapter 4) John is witness to Christ as Righteous Judge with Sovereign power. His worthiness rests on being a sinless Lamb victorious over death.

Glossary of Imagery by Verse for Revelation 5

v. 1	scroll	(Daniel 7:13-14) title deed to earth and all that is in it (Psalm 2:7-9) perhaps the new covenant God makes with Israel (Jeremiah 31:31, 33) (Romans 11:26:27) and fulfills God's covenant with Abraham (Genesis 12:2-3) Christ to repossess a dirty residence - clean-up is needed (Judgment)
v. 1	both sides	the scroll was full - no more could be added
v. 1	seven seals	seven programs for renovation (Judgment) may have some significance with Roman legal customs
v. 2	mighty angel	notable angel - perhaps Gabriel - name means 'Strength of God'
v. 5	Lion	full strength and power - capable of fierceness
v. 6	seven horns	perfect power
v. 6	seven eyes	perfect vision
v. 6	seven spirits	perfect wisdom
v. 8	incense	Old Testament practice for prayers of the people reaching God (Psalm 141:2)
v. 9	new song	joyful anticipation - Millennial Reign of Christ (Revelation 20:1-6) another joyful anticipation (Exodus 15:1-2)

Notes for Revelation 5

REVELATION 6
Approaching Hoof Beats - The First Six Judgments

Welcome to Daniel's seventieth week! Even though Israel is not mentioned for a while, <u>She is back in the picture</u>. Events going forward eventually affects God's chosen people. The white horse here is not the white horse of chapter nineteen!

Read Revelation 6:1-8

1) From the symbols given in vv. 1-2, would you say the rider on the white horse seeks victory through military conquest or negotiations? Explain....

2) From vv. 3-4, what changes in society would be necessary for murder to be as common as relational arguments?

Discussion:

Politics aside, do you think the proliferation of military assault weapons into residential neighborhoods will eventually contribute to the prophecy of vv. 3-4? What changes in society has facilitated road-rage to becoming more deadly?

3) What does history tell us how life in America was from 1929 to 1933?

4) a. Read and describe the scene in Lamentations 4:8-10.

   b. Do you think such a dire situation will ever exist in America?

5) In reference to the fourth seal, we most likely must include micro-organisms. What diseases are with us in today's world that could prove to be catastrophic if the world supply of vaccines were limited?

6) Might there be diseases on the horizon that are not with us today?

Read Revelation 6:9-17

7) Those who had been murdered for their faith cried out for judgment and vengeance against their murderers. They were given a white robe and told:

   a. to avenge themselves with the aid of the four horsemen.

   b. that it was unchristian to demand vengeance.

   c. wait a while longer until a certain number of martyred is reached.

   d. pray.

8) Compare and explain vv. 15-16 with Genesis 3:8.

Discussion:

Out of what time period do you think these martyrs are from? Old Testament saints, the Church age, Tribulation saints or might they simply represent people of all ages who were martyred for their testimony of Jesus Christ? See Acts 7:54-66

9) How is the sixth seal different from the first five?

10) What did Jesus reveal about His power? See Matthew 8:23-27

11) Suggest the thinking of people not wishing to see the return of Christ?

12) What will unbelievers come to realize when Christ returns?

Discussion:

What is the difference between vindictive judgment and righteous judgment?

Optional: Using a dictionary, write the definition of paradox.

Summary Statement:

Chapter six is a paradox! All the fury of God is unleashed by a Lamb!

> *Therefore, you kings, be wise; Be warned, you rulers of the earth.*
> *Serve the Lord with fear and rejoice with trembling.*
> *Kiss the Son, lest He be angry and you be destroyed in your way,*
> *For His wrath can flare up in a moment.*
> *Blessed are all who take refuge in Him"*
> Psalm 2:10-12

This chapter is the official start of Daniel's seventieth week. Christ's return is still seven years away. Think of these eighty-four months as forty-two plus forty-two. As stated earlier, when the Church is taken up, the world will not yet visually see Christ but they are going to experience His Judgment for seven years.

The Gentle Carpenter is initiating His presence for seven reasons; **One:** Fulfill remaining prophesies' of the prophets; **Two:** Fulfill remaining covenants; **Three:** Avenge those who had wronged His people; *"It is mine to avenge, I will repay, their day of disaster in near and their doom rushes upon them."* (Deuteronomy 32:35) **Four:** Judge the nations; **Five:** Redeem Israel as He is recognized as Messiah; **Six:** Destroy the apostate church, rebellious men and the moral abyss of the world system which is called Babylon; **Seven:** Establish His Kingdom.

Time out: Why the necessity for total annihilation? One possible answer: One could hardly conceive Washington, Moscow, Teheran, Rome, Berlin, Paris, Beijing and all state capitols saying, 'come right on in Jesus and take over!' Absolutely not! That is why the world will face an Armageddon upon His return!

Are the fires of hades a real place or just a concept as some say? The answer to that question best not be a matter of a poll at the supermarket! Whether Luke 16:19-31 is a parable or an actual event is a moot point. Jesus would not illustrate a fictional place! Heaven and hell are too important a matter to leave it up to opinions! Tragically, that is what millions choose to do. Jesus was clear in His teachings and the word of this Book is without refute. Many will spend eternity in a fire. Christ came so that mankind had a way of escaping this awful place! People who insist on debating these truths will one day cross over and discover this truth too late!

The evil of the first five seals results when the Holy Spirit departs with the Church. (2 Thessalonians 2:7) The sixth seal is an act of God and not the work of evil men. Know the difference! Also, let us not overlook some inhabitants of heaven are emotionally involved with what they view as slowness on God's part by asking questions of Him. In the coming chapters don't overlook conversations and displays of emotion.

If you already have a perspective on the Judgments, you can build on them. Either confirming your beliefs or being challenged to other possibilities.

<u>Application</u>

"Blessed is he whose transgression is forgiven, whose sin is covered. Blessed is the man to whom the Lord does not impute iniquity, and in whose spirit there is no deceit." "I acknowledged my sin to You, my iniquity I hide not. 'I confessed my transgressions to the Lord,' and You forgave the iniquity of my sin." **(Psalm 32:1-2, 5)**

Glossary of Imagery by Verse for Revelation 6

Note: Symbols being provided to assist your reading. All have been used elsewhere in both Old Testament and New Testament. In the interest of space, their origin is generally omitted.

v. 1	seals	each seal unleashes a new Judgment
v. 2	white horse	symbol of false peace by antichrist (beast of chapter thirteen)
v. 2	bow	weapon of war - absence of arrows implies victory by agreement
v. 2	crown	temporary leader whose victory achieved by insincere promise
v. 4	red horse	bloody time on earth follows after false peace agreement
v. 4	kill each other	lawlessness - old west mentality - proliferation of lethal weapons
v. 4	sword	not the long variety but daggers used for assassination and murder
v. 5	black horse	famine - survival replaces crop growing
v. 5	scales	represents scarcity of food – rationing - food lines
v. 6	quart of wheat	very basic food supply
v. 6	barley	animal food
v. 6	denarius	money in short supply
v. 6	oil-wine	luxury items guarded
v. 8	pale horse	high mortality rate
v. 8	hades	not a concept - but a place predestined for sinners
v. 9	fifth seal	prayers of the martyred for God's vengeance on their murderers
v. 11	number	God's predetermined number of saints to be martyred
v. 12	sixth seal	first five seals is God using men - here God's direct intervention
v. 12	great quake	on a global scale
v. 12	bloody moon	suggests glow from volcanic eruptions discolors the sky
v. 13	stars fell	suggests massive asteroid bombardment
v. 13	late figs	suggests seasonal changes become blurred
v. 14	sky receded	suggests a polluted atmosphere
v. 16	Wrath of the Lamb	people come to realize Christ was no myth
v. 17	Great Day	the sixth seal begins *"the Day of the Lord"*.......

Notes for Revelation 6

Accessing the Scriptures

REVELATION 7
Grace Does Not Take a Rest

Be not afraid, for I have redeemed you. Be not afraid, I've called you by name.
My love for you is ever lasting, my love for you shall have no end.
When you pass through the waters, I will surround you.
When you pass through the floods, they will not sweep over.
When you walk through the fire, you will not be consumed.
You are my child, you are my child, you are so precious to me.

(Hymnal message drawn from Isaiah 43:1-5 Used by permission, www.choirstersguild.org)

This beautiful anthem is appropriate for the second part of this chapter. *"Blessed is the man who perseveres under trial, because when he has stood the test, he will receive the crown of life that God has promised to those who love Him."* (James 1:12) Do avoid zipping through verses four through eight. Consider them carefully as to Israel's history and the Savior Himself as a Descendant from the Tribe of Judah.

Some cults teach they are this group of 144,000, choosing to forget that chapters six through nineteen is solely about God's program for Israel. Do not listen to them!

Read Revelation 7:1-8

1) Even though wind can be destructive, imagine there not being any wind at all for months, even years. What would be the effects of calm winds twenty-four seven?

Author's assistance: Judgment is suspended for a time, perhaps to allow the elect Jews a time of reflection as to the events unfolding in the world. Until now, Israel had not seen Jesus as the one the prophets spoke of. Obviously, that is now changed and Jesus takes a big step in fulfilling Matthew 15:24. See also Matthew 10:5-7

2) From what ethnic group does God seal the 144,000 individuals?

3) 144,000 may seem too large a number to be called a remnant but considering the millions of Jews scattered around the world today that number is but a remnant. Name another instance God set aside a remnant? See 1 Kings 19:9b-10, 18

Read Romans 9:6-16, 11:1-8, 11:11-15, 11:25

4) Are all Jews sons of Abraham?

5) a. By what standard is a man deemed righteous? See Romans 3:16

   b. Write the verse from John 3:16 and state if you believe God.

6) What is God's primary reason for election? (Romans 9:14-16)

7) In the two thousand plus years between the sixty-ninth and seventieth week of Daniel, what occurred? See Romans 11:11-15, 25

Discussion:

Though it is not clear if events of this chapter occur between the sixth and seventh seals or, if they are a description of events that are ongoing during the course of the first six seal Judgments. Most likely they were ongoing. What do you think?

Read Revelation 7:9-17

8) In the news, you and I constantly see the goliaths of society, standout sports figures, politicians and Hollywood celebrities. What does this chapter tell you about who God sees that our news cares little about?

9) What does verse ten tell you about man's ability to good their way to heaven?

10) Using a Bible Dictionary;

   a. Define Grace.

   b. Define Mercy.

   c. How has God exhibited both?

11) Identify various ways saved people show their gratitude to God for their good fortune to be included in God's family?

Summary Statement:

Love and trust is the heart of God's glory! (John 3:16) In the course of God's Wrath, Mercy remains! His promise to His covenant people is front and center. The nameless multitudes of the world take refuge under His tent. (v. 15) Those insignificant others the world has forgotten whom God remembers!

Christ came to earth but His people received Him not. (Romans 9-11) It is difficult for you and me living in the Church Age to conceive of any group giving praise, honor and worship to Christ other than the Church. But this chapter relates that after centuries of rejecting Christ as the Messiah, a large number of Jews will accept Jesus. We see the *first fruits* of a redeemed Israel. Perhaps events unfolding on earth have given them a new perspective on truth.

To suite their own delusions, some religious sects have distorted the identity of the 144,000. Please, the Scripture identifies them as Jews! Let God say what He wants to say! The only way this group can be anyone other than Jews is by rewriting the Scriptures which is heresy. (Revelation 22:18-19) <u>The rewriting of God's word is not OK. Rewriting of Scripture is always done by a founder who claims new revelations from God.</u> These individuals are pure and simple, apostates! They are among the false prophets that occupy our landscape today. (Matthew 7:15) Apostates are sent strong delusions to distort the Scriptures. Their purpose is to test the resolve of us who regard the Word of God as unalterable. Tragically, millions follow after these false prophets to their destruction. Beloved, there is only One founder, One Word, One Revelation and it is Christ as recorded by witness of the Apostles in the four Gospels.

In the second part of this chapter, verse thirteen jumps out! An elder asks John who the people of verse nine are. The exchange between John and the elder gives further evidence <u>the Church will not experience the Tribulation</u>. If the Multitude here were the Church, John would identify them as such. Neither can this Multitude be just Old Testament Jews because <u>they represent all nations</u>. That leaves only two possibilities, these are a gathering of those who have come out of the Great Tribulation. Additionally, this study takes the position that God in His Mercy does not exclude those who never heard the Gospel such as inhabitants of remote areas on earth. The Apostle Paul addresses these folks in Romans 1:20. You and I must not be narrow in considering the breadth of God's Mercy! *"Is God unjust? Not at all! For He says to Moses, "I will have mercy on whom I have mercy, and I will have compassion on whom I have compassion." It does not, therefore, depend on man's desire or effort, but on God's mercy."* (Romans 9:14-16)

<u>Application</u>

Develop a concept of a present heaven and the existence of distinguishable life forms there. Unknown individuals are introduced here. See John 10:16

Glossary of Imagery by Verse for Revelation 7

v. 1	four corners	total coverage of the earth
v. 2	seal	whom God seals is forever His
v. 4	144,000	Redeemed Jews in God's service replaces work of the Church are the *"first fruits"* of a Redeemed Israel (Zechariah 12:10) New Testament renewal of Jeremiah 2:3
v. 4	all tribes	all Twelve Tribes equally represented offer a clue to election
v. 9	multitude	During Tribulation, those who missed Rapture have one final test of faith. In the face of certain death, they reject the temptation to take the mark of the beast which is 666. (Revelation 13:16-18)
v. 14	Tribulation	great wickedness - unparalleled distress - also a time of Grace (Matthew 24:12-14)
v. 15	Temple-tent	In the Old Testament, only Levites were permitted in the presence of God. Now people of all nations and tongues can come to Him.

Notes for Revelation 7

Accessing the Scriptures

REVELATION 8
The Lord Turns Up the Heat

The trumpet had little role in the life of the early Church but it played a huge role in both Hebrew life and worship. The same can be said of the objects of the Tabernacle. Their role was part of Old Testament law. This chapter is one of many that is Israel focused. God is about the business of fulfilling numerous covenants with His people.

Read Revelation 8:1-5

1) What kind of reaction would you exhibit if you observed a diver about to jump from a thirty story cliff into a body of water below?

2) To spare you the burden of running all over the early books of the law in the Old Testament, read Hebrews 9:1-12. Explain the difference between the prayers of the people in the Old Testament and the prayers of the people in the New Testament.

3) Read Numbers 10:1-9, Joshua 6:2, 4-5, 20 and Isaiah 27:12-13

   a. Of what use was the trumpet to the Hebrews of the Old Testament?

   b. As you study the trumpet Judgments, what process is unfolding in regard to God's covenant people?

Discussion:
Your glossary suggests that the trumpets are symbolic of commands that have the impact of the powerful sound trumpets produce. This study holds to the belief that actual trumpets will not be seen or heard just as four horses (chapter 6) will not be seen riding across the sky. You are free to discuss if the symbols of trumpets and horses are literal or symbolic. Symbolic or not, does it really matter?

4) The prayers of the saints is recorded. (v. 3) What might those prayers be addressing?
   See Matthew 6:9-13

5) What had been the prayers of the Tribulation martyrs? See Revelation 6:9-11

6) Would you say the purpose of prayer is to have God's will on earth or God's will in heaven?

Read Revelation 8:6-13

7) What percentage of the earth is affected by the first four trumpet Judgments?

8) Suggest a reason why God just simply doesn't destroy all evil on earth in one cataclysmic event and get it over with.

9) What characteristic of God does delay represent?

10) What message does the talking eagle announce?

11) What does the symbol of the eagle suggest is going to occur on earth?
     See Matthew 24:28, Revelation 19:17-18

12) What is the fate of those who refused to come to the knowledge of God?
     See 2 Thessalonians 1:6-9

Summary Statement:

"Blow the trumpet in Zion; sound the alarm on my holy hill. Let all who live in the land tremble, for the day of the Lord is coming. It is close at hand – a day of darkness and gloom, a day of clouds and blackness. Like dawn spreading across the mountains a large and mighty army comes, such as never was of old nor ever will be in ages to come." (Joel 2:1-2)

 **Leader's Helicopter Overview for Revelation 8**
(Optional or Prepare Your Own)

When Christ opens the seventh seal, we get a picture of unprecedented fury upon the earth. Seven trumpet Judgments segue to the seven bowl judgments. If it seems bad now, things are just heating up!

From the questions and discussions, one must come to the conclusion, God is preparing the way for His covenant people to live in a world free of anti- Semitism. When Joshua and Caleb went into the land of milk and honey (Joshua 6:20) they fully expected God to deliver the land to them and God did! <u>And He is going to do it again.</u> This time, all who love the Lord will live in a world of milk and honey.

Application

Perhaps an attitude adjustment! Are you one of those who says to himself or herself, how can a loving God be so destructive and violent? Then ask yourself this question, <u>can a Holy God remain Holy if He is not Just</u>? Of His Just nature, God provided ample warning in His Word and by those He has sent into the world including Jesus. Did He not offer to pardon all men in Christ, who after all, suffered on a cross, laying down His life for all? The warning has been there for two thousand years. It will end badly for those who reject the righteousness God freely provided in His Son.

Review

<u>Event</u>	<u>Chapter</u>
The Apostle John, imprisoned on the island Patmos. Empowered by the Holy Spirit, John sees his friend and Master. Jesus, now Glorified and positioned to evaluate the Church.	1
Christ reveals the condition of the Church.	2 & 3
Jesus grants John visual access to the present heaven. John observes heaven and all creation is represented. A scroll is introduced. Only Christ is worthy to unseal it.	4 & 5
Christ opens six of seven seal Judgments. First four seals gives John visions; *antichrist* (white horse) *war* (red horse) *famine* (black horse) *death* (pale horse) Fifth seal reveals Old Testament/Church martyrs. Sixth seal reveals acts of nature/God breathed.	6
144,000 Jews are sealed from the ongoing Judgments. Introduction of a multitude of Tribulation saints.	7
Seventh seal reveals seven trumpet Judgments. Four strike the earth in the form of natural disasters/acts of God. Golden Censer is introduced.	8

Glossary of Imagery by Verse for Revelation 8

v. 1	seventh seal	gateway to seven trumpet Judgments (8:7-9:21, 11:15-19)
v. 1	silence	great anticipation of what is coming
v. 1	half-hour	first six seals came rapidly - pause here is short
v. 2	seven angels	not angels in the usual sense - angels of Judgment
v. 2	seven trumpets	seven authorities with commands with the force of a trumpet
v. 3	censer	represents prayers of Old Testament saints
v. 4	prayers of the saints	prayers of New Testament saints
v. 5	filled with fire	the anger of the Lord in full bloom
v. 6	sounded his trumpet	execution of this Judgment with great force
v. 7	fire – hail - blood	volcanic eruptions conjoin with hail kills millions
v. 8	mountains into sea	volcanos collapse into the sea taking lava with it
v. 10	great star	asteroid breaks into thousands of pieces falling into water supply
v. 11	wormwood	a ghastly tasting plant - often toxic
v. 12	sun darkens	result of volcanic clouds
v. 13	three woes	one for the three remaining trumpet Judgments

Notes for Revelation 8

Accessing the Scriptures

REVELATION 9
Divine Judgment, Two Woes, Stubborn Unrepentance

The fifth trumpet (first Woe) is quickly followed by the sixth trumpet. (Second Woe) The chapter reveals apocalyptic scenes. There is a remarkable resemblance here to Amos 5-7 where we read of God seeking to draw a response of repentance, administered Divine punishment upon Israel.

Read Revelation 9:1-12

1) a. What kind of life form do locusts normally destroy?

   b. What kind of life form do the locusts destroy here? (v. 4)

2) When the destroyer passed over Egypt killing the first born of every man and animal, what was it that spared God's people from death?

3) What is the mark which God seals His people with in verse four?

4) Regarding Judgment, what has God done in the past and what is He planning to do in the future? See 2 Peter 3:6-7

5) What is God's track record in regard to sin? See 2 Peter 2:4-6

6) Describe how a righteous man views the world. See 2 Peter 2:7-8

7) Describe how unrighteous men live life. See 2 Peter 2:10-14

8) a. How does God view unscrupulous people? See 2 Peter 2:17

    b. What has God reserved for them?

Discussion:

The phrase *once saved always saved* is accepted as truth by many. Others say salvation can be lost. Read 2 Peter 2:20-22, John 10:27-30, Romans 8:28-31. What is your conclusion?

Read Revelation 9:13-21

9) If an angel has been bound, what kind of angel must he be?

Discussion:

The invading army of 200 million (v. 16) would have us believe these to be actual men on horseback. Given the advancement in modern warfare this seems highly unlikely. As we read on (v. 17) it seems more likely John is using natural language to describe either a plague or a supernatural invasion. Verses eighteen and twenty actually use the word plague. What do you think?

10) What effects do you anticipate the drug culture will have in the future?

11) Do you think same sex marriage will one day be acceptable worldwide? Why?

12) In the face of obvious Divine Judgment, what was the response of ungodly men in this chapter?

13) Why do you think evil men refuse to give up their way of living and seek God?

Summary Statement:

Some men simply love the world system too much to ever turn from it. They love it so much they are willing to perish for it. (v. 20)

"Still they did not repent of the works of their hands." (v. 20) Biblically, the word repent has to do with changing one's direction, a way of thinking if you will. Jesus spoke these wise words, *"Seek first the kingdom of God and His righteousness."* (Matthew 6:33) *"Do not store up for yourselves treasure on earth, where moth and rust destroy, and where thieves break in and steal. But store up for yourselves treasures in heaven, where moth and rust do not destroy and where thieves do not break in and steal. For where your treasure is, there your heart will be also."* (Matthew 6:19-21)

John speaks of 200 million mounted troops in this chapter. Later in chapter sixteen, he speaks of military forces in the area of the Euphrates River preparing for the battle of Armageddon. This study takes the position these two events are unrelated. The army of this chapter comes out of the trumpet Judgments. The armies of chapter sixteen come out of the bowl Judgments which have yet to occur. Conclusion, the 200 million grotesque looking mounted troops in this chapter is imagery of horrific plagues. In fact, the term plague is used twice.

"There is a way that seems right to a man, but in the end it leads to death"

Your discussion questions included how a drug culture can have effects on humankind. Drug influence creates an altered state of mind. We can be sure, an altered mind doesn't include bending one's knee to Christ. People under the influence of drugs evidently experience things outside normal human experiences. This is nothing less than sorcery. The Scriptures are too full of condemnation of sorcery to list them.

"At the beginning the Creator made them male and female, and said, for this reason a man will leave his father and mother and be united to his wife, and the two will become one flesh." (Matthew 19:4-5) Can Jesus' words be more clear? If God intended Joe and Bill becoming one flesh wouldn't Jesus have included this to the Pharisee? Using love as window dressing to justify same-sex unions perverts God's gift of love and deceives those who do. Moral and religious deception is on the rise. Some Churches already perform same-sex unions. Citing love regarding same-sex marriage is a moral deception. We shall address religious deception in coming chapters.

Application

"Be strong in the Lord and in His mighty power. Put on the full armor of God so that you can take your stand against the devil's schemes." (Ephesians 6:10-11) One who lives for the here and now, had better suck up all they can! It is all they are going to get! If materialism is your love, there is time. Put Christ first! *"Whoever of you does not forsake all that he has cannot be my disciple."* (Luke 14:33)

Glossary of Imagery by Verse for Revelation 9

v. 1	fallen star	Satan (Isaiah 14:12, 2 Corinthians 11:14, Revelation 12:7-9)
v. 1	abyss	same place the rich man was in as described in the Parable (Luke 16:19-31) place of torment adjacent to the lake of fire Sheol, hades - lost souls go here until Revelation 20:14 at which time they are thrown into the lake of fire
v. 3	locusts	a special kind of being having the ability to take orders
v. 7	crowns	suggest these locust type beings have great power to harm
v. 9	breastplates	suggest that flesh is no match against iron-like aggressors
v. 11	abyss angel	the leader of the army of locusts
v. 12	woe	this one is the fifth trumpet Judgment
v. 13	horns	a powerful group who serve at God's direction
v. 14	four angels	Since these angels are bound, they are fallen angels capable of inflicting great harm.
v. 14	Euphrates	use here is significant - a prophesied event (Armageddon)
v. 16	army	two possibilities - World War, East vs. West or most likely, a massive plague. Either way, the result will be horrific.
v. 20	demons	Men's lusts for money, power and pleasure.

Notes for Revelation 9

Accessing the Scriptures

REVELATION 10
The Angel and the Little Scroll

This chapter gives the appearance of a timeout between the sixth and seventh trumpet Judgments just as chapter seven appeared to be a time out between the sixth and seventh seal Judgments. This study takes the position these Judgments are ongoing. John is simply taking literary breaks to describe other events.

Read Revelation 10:1-7

1) What is your personal assessment of the authority of this mighty angel?

2) Do you think this is the same angel as the angel in chapter 5:2? Explain.

3) Some say the angel in this chapter is Christ. Why is this not Christ? (vv. 5-6)

4) Compare the face of this angel with the face of Moses. See Exodus 34:29

5) Describe the face of Stephen as he spoke to the Sanhedrin about Jesus.
   See Acts 6:19

Read Revelation 10:8-11

Many scriptures relate that God's Word is sweet to the taste of a believer. (See Jeremiah 15:16, Ezekiel 3:1-3, Psalm 119:103) In regard to the unbeliever, the Apostle writes; *"The message of the cross is foolishness to those who are perishing."* (1 Corinthians 1:18) Even among al-a-carte believers, some Scriptures can often cause them indigestion.

6) Compare John's instructions (vv. 8-11) with the prophet Ezekiel's instructions.
   See Ezekiel 2:9-3:4

Discussion:

Why do you think the Word of God would be upsetting to John? What are some other reasons Scripture make people uneasy?

7) It is not unusual for Scripture to evoke a variety of emotions. Write a brief emotional response to the following scriptures:

"The Lord is my shepherd, I shall not want." (Psalm 23:1)

"Bless those who curse you, pray for those who mistreat you." (Luke 6:28)

"Hear my cry for mercy as I call to you for help, as I lift up my hands toward your Most Holy Place." (Psalm 28:2)

"I urge, then, first of all, that requests, prayers, intercession and thanksgiving be made for everyone – For kings and all those in authority." (1 Timothy 2:1-2)

"Father, into your hands I commit My Spirit." (Luke 23:46)

"If anyone comes to Me and does not hate his father and mother, his wife and children, his brothers and sister – yes, even his own life – he cannot be my disciple." (Luke 18:22)

"When He had received the drink, Jesus said, 'It is finished.'" (John 19:30)

Discussion:

How does *"It is finished"* relate to separating Grace and legalism? [See Romans 6:14]

Summary Statement:

John's reaction to the little scroll can mean earth is coming under Judgment. Great suffering lies ahead. His stomach churns as he must prophesy against many, just as the prophets of old had experienced regarding Israel centuries earlier.

A two-legged being standing with one foot on the land and the other on the sea is a bit off the wall. But it is with hyperbole John makes his point. What better way to illustrate <u>God's Sovereignty over men and nations</u> than the literary style John uses in this chapter? Jesus often used hyperbole to make a point! Luke 18:22 is an example; *"to hate his mother and father, his wife and his children, his brother and sister, even his own life."* This is of course hyperbole to put the Lord first in one's life. I.e. The Church at Ephesus (Revelation 2:4) had become complacent with God's fundamental commandment. *"Love the Lord your God with all your heart and with all your soul and with all your mind. This is the first and greatest commandment."* (Matthew 22:37-38)

John was familiar with the Ten Plagues of Egypt, so it is no wonder the contents of the little scroll gave him pause. The coming Judgments were going to make the Ten Plagues of Egypt look like a bad cold. Worse, John is given the job to communicate to humankind the coming horror of the seventh trumpet and the accompanying holocaust of the bowl Judgments.

You and I generally give little thought to the unseen world of angels and demons yet they appear frequently in the Bible. The angel here is not Christ as some suggest. Verses five and six attests to this. The angel is however, God's advance man. He has come to claim the land and the sea for Christ. His first order of business is to answer this question; *"How long, Sovereign Lord, until you judge the inhabitants of the earth and avenge our blood?" – "They were told to wait a little longer, until the number of their fellow servants were to be killed as they had been."* (Revelation 6:10-11) *"There will be no more delay!"* (v. 6) Obviously the prescribed number of Gentiles to be martyred has been reached! <u>This chapter concludes the first forty-two months of Tribulation.</u> (See Daniel 7:25, a time = 1 yr. + times = 2 yrs. + half a time = 6 months, a total of 42 months)

Application

We cannot suppose to know all the mysteries of creation or why God permits what He does. What we do know is where we can rest our wits, who to trust to see us thru. Perhaps that is why evil is permitted, so that we may see the power of God overcome it and see His people through it.

God Makes a Way for His People
The Lord works in ways unseen by us; Remember, He was there at the edge of a sea.
When His Children faced their darkest hour. In love, in strength, He released His power.
If you also, His Child, are about to take a frightful step!
Wait! He is there, take His hand and be bold! He will make a way.
(Based on Isaiah 43:19)

Glossary for Imagery by Verse for Revelation 10

v. 1	mighty angel	not Christ
v. 1	cloud	splendor of His place of origin
v. 1	rainbow	covenant God made to never again use a flood in Judgment (See glossary Revelation 4:3)
v. 2	sea - land	This angel is Christ's real estate agent if you will. Christ has already claimed title deed to Earth (Revelation 5) This angel has come to announce the Word of God is Supreme
v. 3	seven thunders	perfect commands of the Spirit of God (Psalm 29:34)
v. 4	seal up	not the same as Revelation 22:10 - just as it was with Daniel (Daniel 12:9) What is sealed here, no man is to know. It is a mystery of God.
v. 7	mystery	This study offers possibilities only. That Israel and the Church are united into one body. Why God permitted evil. Why God permitted suffering. The revealing of who are the sheep and goats (Matthew 25:31-32) God is no longer a mystery to unbelievers.
v. 8	scroll	not the same scroll of chapter five - that scroll was the title deed to earth - This scroll is to be eaten, therefore it is the Word of God. (Jeramiah 15:16, Ezekiel 3:1-3, Psalm 119:103)
v. 11	prophesy	to let John know there is more to come... ...

Notes for Revelation 10

Accessing the Scriptures

REVELATION 11
Two Witnesses and the Seventh Trumpet

This chapter has multiple themes. Verses one through twelve is a continuation of chapter ten. Material within the second woe is inserted. (The sixth trumpet judgment). Verses thirteen and fourteen concludes the destruction which began in Revelation 9:13-21. The seventh trumpet ushers in the third woe but its execution doesn't begin until Revelation 12:9-12.

Read Revelation 11:1-2

1) What is Jesus' prophecy concerning Jerusalem at the end of the age?
    See Luke 21:20-24

2) In the learned Christian's mind, what nation comes to mind with the terms Temple, Holy of Holies, Olive tree and Sackcloth?

3) What does a Lampstand represent to you as a Christian?

Read Revelation 11:3-14

4) At the Transfiguration, who were the two individuals who appeared with Jesus?
    See Matthew 17:3

5) At the Ascension of Jesus, two men dressed in white appeared on the scene and stood beside the Apostles. What is different about these two men with the two men at the Transfiguration? See Acts 1:9-10

6) How does Scripture instruct believers to witness? See Deuteronomy 19:15 and Matthew 18:16

7) The two unnamed witnesses are associated with sackcloth, lampstands and olive trees. Would you say this is representative of two believing Jews or two Tribulation Gentiles?

8) What powers did God grant the two witnesses?

Discussion:
As you read the account of the two witnesses, do you think it is really important to identify who they are and perhaps even be able to name them?

9) Which verse in this chapter do you think best glorifies and exemplifies the power of God and why?

10) What does the murder of God's two witnesses and leaving their bodies lying in the street for all to see tell you where this world is heading?

11) a. How does the second woe end?

b. What is the effect of the earthquake in verse thirteen? [See Glossary]

Read Revelation 11:15-17
Note: Translation of verse seventeen is best read from the NKJV Bible. (Copyright 1982 by Thomas Nelson) *"We give You thanks, O Lord God Almighty. The One who is and who was and who is to come"* This is a better match to Revelation 1:8 NIV.

12) *"If those day had not been cut short, no one would survive, but for the sake of the elect those days will be shortened."* (Matthew 24:22) The Church is no longer on earth, so who are these elect? See Revelation 7:3-4

Discussion:
Verse nineteen uses the verb <u>was,</u> meaning that during the Tribulation period, God opens heaven for people on earth to see. Do you think all people on earth will view heaven or will this be limited to the 144,000 of chapter seven?

Summary Statement:
The power of God, the plan of God, the trustworthiness of God are all on display in this chapter. The leaving of bodies purposefully lying in the street accentuates the depravity of a godless world.

Leader's Helicopter Overview for Revelation 11
(Optional or Prepare Your Own)

John inserts this material between the second and third woe. The material is unrelated to his account of the ongoing death and destruction taking place. But it is relevant to the direction he is taking us. The Apostle Paul does somewhat the same thing in Romans nine through eleven where he inserts Israel's history in the middle of his dissertation on doctrine and application. Check and see how the end of Romans eight segues quite nicely to Romans twelve.

Two issues emerge here! Do we spiritualize the Temple in verse one? If we do, we create unresolvable problems! This study takes the position a third Temple will be built! Without it, Daniel's prophecy and repeated by Jesus, *"the abomination that causes desolation"* (Matthew 24:15, Daniel 10:25, 11:31) cannot be fulfilled. In today's political climate, a rebuilt Temple seems unlikely, yet in the economy of God the unexpected happens! The second issue is the time represented here. Is this the first forty-two months of the Tribulation or the second? This study takes the position it is the first forty-two months but we won't be dogmatic about it! For certain, anytime you see Temple used, Israel is in the picture! The Church is never identified with a physical temple. (A building) [See 1 Corinthians 6:19 and Ephesians 2:21-22] Temples exist today but rest assured, these are apostate temples.

A visit to the old city of Jerusalem today reveals a city of multiple cultures who have built religious structures all over the place. Verse two lets us know at the mid- point of the Tribulation these cultures have forty-two months remaining to have their way in God's city.

When a person is preparing to occupy a new dwelling, they measure it! John's measuring of the Temple is symbolic that a new tenant will be taking possession and the new tenant is Christ! Rod represents comfort for God's people, *"thy rod and Thy staff they comfort me."* (Psalm 23:4) But also, rod represents punishment for the enemies of Christ *"You shall break them with a rod of iron; You shall dash them to pieces like a potter's vessel."* (Psalm 2:10) Those who plunder the Temple of God in this life, will have no place in it in the next life! J. Vernon McGee writes that the gift giving in verse ten is the devil's Christmas!

At the pronouncement of the seventh trumpet Judgment, the twenty-four Elders (The Church) break into worship and celebration.

Application

Verses eight through ten reveal the cold barbaric nature of the last days. The Mardi-Gras of that period you don't want to be a part of should it come in your life time. Apply The Parable of the Ten Virgins to your life! [Read Matthew 25:1-13]

Glossary of Imagery by Verse for Revelation 11

v. 1	reed - rod	comfort for believers (Psalm 23:4) punishment for unbelievers (Psalm 2:9-10)
v. 2	outer court	symbolic/the plundering hordes will not be a part of the Kingdom
v. 2	trample the Holy City	antichrist institutes *"the abomination that brings desolation"* (Matthew 24:15, Daniel 10:25, 11:31)
v. 7	beast	antichrist (see Revelation 13)
v. 8	great city	Jerusalem
v. 12	ascended in a cloud	seeing this has no effect on obstinate people (see Luke 16:31)
v. 13	earthquake	confined to Jerusalem as was the earthquake when Jesus was crucified - Israel redeemed here. (Romans 11:25-27)
v. 19	lightning – rumblings – thunder	impending Judgments - more to come... ....

Notes for Revelation 11

THE TIMING OF A HOLY GOD'S JUSTICE

*"It is good that one should hope and wait quietly for the
salvation of the Lord."* (Lamentations 3:26 NKJV)

Christian author and writer, James Banks includes in His book, "Praying the Prayers
of the Bible," fitting notes to inspire us to take heart. Evil men have their way now, but
in the end, God will have His way:

*I'm sorry for envying the wicked. ---

I almost lost my footing. My feet were slipping, and I was almost gone. For I envied
the arrogant when I saw them prosper despite their wickedness. They seem to live
such painless lives; their bodies are so healthy and strong. They don't have troubles
like other people; they're not plagued with problems like everyone else. They wear
arrogance like a jeweled necklace and clothe themselves with cruelty. These fat cats
have everything their flesh craves! They scoff and speak only evil; in arrogance they
seek to crush others. They boast against the very heavens, and their words strut
throughout the earth. Look at these wicked people – enjoying a life of ease while their
riches multiply. So I tried to understand why the wicked prosper. But what a difficult
task it is! Then I went into Your sanctuary, O God, and I finally understood the destiny
of the wicked. Truly, you put them on a slippery path and send them sliding over the
cliff to destruction. In an instant they are destroyed, completely swept away by terrors.
When you arise, O Lord, You will laugh at their silly ideas as a person laughs at dreams
in the morning. Then I realized that my heart was bitter, and I was all torn up inside. I
was so foolish and ignorant – I must have seemed like a senseless animal to You. Yet I
still belong to You; You hold my right hand. You guide me with Your counsel, leading
me to a glorious destiny. Drawn from Psalm 73:2-9, 12, 16-24

*James Banks, Praying the Prayers of the Bible®. 2013 by Discovery House Publishing © Grand Rapids, MI. Reprinted by Permission All
Rights Reserved. Discovery House Publishing P.O. Box 3566 Grand Rapids, MI 49501 ISBN 978-1-57293-750-5

REVELATION 12
The Woman and the Dragon

The scope and magnitude of Satan's wickedness comes into focus. It is vital to identify the woman correctly. She is Israel! To identify her any other way would detour your study and give rise to extraordinary unexplainable issues! The third woe (Revelation 11:14) is initiated in verse nine and identified in verse twelve. This chapter offers the challenge of looking ahead to future events which Revelation is about. While at the same time, having to deal with events that have already occurred.

Read Revelation 12:1

1) Who is protecting who, day and night in verse one? [Read Nehemiah 4:1-9] See also Exodus 13:20-21

2) Let's examine the forensics and identify the woman correctly. Let us connect these dots to assist our identification. From Joseph's dream, what can we associate with the following? See Genesis 37:9-10

   a. the sun   _____   _____

   b. the moon   _____   _____

   c. the stars   _____   _____

3) What had happened to Jerusalem five hundred years before Christ?
   See Daniel 1:1-2

4) Why would Satan not want the Jews to return to Jerusalem and restore that great city? See John 19:25, 30, Matthew 28:5-6

5) Satan obstructs God and people in ways we cannot see. Describe one such obstruction Daniel records. See Daniel 10:12-13

Read Revelation 12:2-6

6) Name some times when Satan attempted to block the redemptive work of Christ. (v. 4) See Matthew 2:16, Nehemiah 4:1-9

7) Select one: Where does a Christian take refuge from Satan?

    a. church congregation   b. a denomination   c. Jesus   d. any religion   e. karma

Read Revelation 12:7-12

8) Verse eight indicates Satan had lost his place in heaven permanently. What had been Satan's purpose in heaven? See Zechariah 3:1-2, Job 1:6-12

Read Revelation 12:13-17

9) During the *"The time of Jacob's trouble"* (Jeremiah 30:7-8) what is God's Covenant People assured of?

10) The symbol of an eagle assures Israel that God will deliver them. What assures you as a Christian that God will deliver you? See Romans 8:38-39

Discussion:

Wilderness/desert, (v. 14) was purposely omitted from the glossary because it was simply too speculative to make a defendable identification. Some think it will be another Diaspora for the Jews while others think the Jews will flee Jerusalem to the Jordan valley in the area of Petra or even south to the Sinai. If you are in a class, give this a few minutes for each other's opinions.

Summary Statement:

The final forty-two months before the return of Christ, the world will experience evil beyond anything ever experienced. Expect anti-Semitism to be global! *"If the Lord had not cut short those days, no one would survive!"* (Mark 13:20)

The seventh trumpet (Revelation 11:15) ushers in the seven bowl Judgments. (Rev. 15-16) But before John prophesies the bowl Judgments, he describes the unseen conflict between good and evil in the heavenly realms. Paul relates a similar picture in Ephesians *"For our struggle is not against flesh and blood, but against the rulers, the authorities, against the powers of this dark world and against the spiritual forces of evil in the heavenly realms."* (Ephesians 6:12)

If you don't identify the Woman as Israel you have your work cut out for you explaining Daniel's prophecy! Further, some interpret verse nine as past but can we say John's narrative suddenly becomes historical? This study takes the position that verse nine is future. Furthermore, verse twelve identifies verse nine as the catalyst for the third woe! Until verse nine, Satan was never fully cut off from access to God! (Job 1, Zechariah 3:1-2) But with the Church now in heaven, his accusing days have ended. (1 Thessalonians 4:16-17, Revelation 3:10) With time on his hands, Satan turns His full fury against Israel and all human creation. Fortunately, only forty-two months remain for him to pursue Israel and her offspring. (Tribulation saints)

Israel will now experience unprecedented anti-Semitism. It is the time referred to as; *"the time of Jacob's trouble."* (Jeremiah 30:7) With the Church removed, one can figure nations that once had Israel's back will now turn against her.

On the topic of *"war in heaven,"* (v. 7) we mortals give little thought to angels or demons. But if we believe the accounts of Jesus, His life and His ministry, neither angels nor demons can be ignored. Ephesians 6:6:10-12 not only implies the existence of demons, it takes them for granted! It was angels who announced the birth of Jesus. (Luke 2:9-15) Scripture lists them some eighty times with most being in the New Testament. Wherever demons appear in Scripture they are never passive. They always have a negative effect on people.

Satan's limited access to God as identified in parts of this lesson now ends. He sets his sights full time on the inhabitants of the earth. Those who hate the Jew he uses to make war against Israel. Satan's full time presence on earth is manifested in the next chapter with the beast out of the sea.

Application

Even though we may not understand all the details of this alarming chapter, we can be sure God will see His covenant people through the perilous time when the evil one unleashes his full fury against Her.

Glossary of Imagery by Verse for Revelation 12

v. 1	woman	Israel
v. 1	sun - moon	identifies the Woman is Israel - She is protected day and night
v. 1	crown of twelve stars	Twelve Tribes or Twelve Apostles
v. 2	pregnant	about Israel revealing Jesus as the Messiah - not about a pregnant Mary awaiting Jesus' birth, please
v. 2	give birth	the Second Coming of Christ - not His birth in Bethlehem as some errantly believe - John is prophesying a future event, not revisiting Jesus' birth to Mary in Bethlehem
v. 2	pain	centuries of pain Israel has suffered waiting for Messiah to come (Isaiah 40:1-11)
v. 3	red dragon	Satan - red represents much bloodshed lies ahead
v. 3	seven heads - ten horns - seven diadems...	world influences under Satan's control
v. 4	- - - - - - - - -	Represents more than opposing the birth of Jesus to Mary in Bethlehem. Satan put up obstacles to the renovation of Jerusalem after the Babylonian exile. (Nehemiah 4:1-9) Satan tried to have the infant Jesus killed by decree of Herod. (Matthew 2:16) Finally, the forces of Satan will face off with Christ at Armageddon (Rev. 16:16)
v. 5	male child	Christ
v. 5	iron scepter	See Psalm 2:9-10
v. 6	desert	place of refuge both spiritual and physical - The Christian world has been God's instrument to protect Israel in the present age.
v. 6	1260 days	definite reference to future events of Daniel's seventieth week a time = one yr. + times = two yrs. + half time = six months (Daniel 7:25) here represents second half of Tribulation when antichrist ends a false peace with Israel and sets himself up in the Temple at Jerusalem *"The abomination that brings desolation"* (Revelation 20:4, Matthew 24:15, Daniel 9:27)
v. 9	Satan cast out	Satan's limited access to God ends (Job 1:6-12, Zech. 3:12, Rev. 12:10)
v. 11	blood of Lamb	Satan's accusations against Christians rejected (Romans 8:33-39)
v. 14	eagle's wings	not a bird or an airplane but that God protects Israel (Exodus 19:4)
v. 14	time - times - half times...	same as verse six, forty two months or 1260 days
v. 16	earth opened her mount	armies coming against Israel are promised the same end Pharaoh's forces experienced (Exodus 14:23-28)
v. 17	rest of her offspring	remaining Tribulation saints who come to Christ

REVELATION 13
The Dragon and Two Beasts

A reading of Daniel 9:25-27 is a prerequisite to comprehend this chapter with any degree of accuracy! Connecting dots is always recommended in Bible study. Also, Daniel 11:36-39 is useful for additional insight about this fellow we call antichrist.

Read Revelation 13:1-10

1) What does the sea represent? See Isaiah 57:20

2) Compare the appearance of the individual John sees here in verses one through three with the appearance of the individual he sees in Revelation 1:13-16.

3) a. Who is the person revealed in Revelation 1? _____

   b. Who is the person revealed here in chapter 13:1-10? _____

4) In relation to one of the heads (a world power) suffering a fatal wound, what world power that once was strong and fell would amaze you if it again reemerged as a world power?

Discussion:

[Read Revelation 13:11-18] Using the known to understand the unknown, what might be some reasons this chapter pictures Satan standing on the shore of the sea?

5) What significant event occurred to make complete the Trinity of God on earth? See Acts 1:4-8

6) Compare the individual described here in verses eleven and twelve to the individual in Deuteronomy 18:14-15, Matthew 3:1.

   a. How are they alike?

   b. How are they different?

7) What was the principle goal of the beast out of the earth? (v. 12)

8) What had been the mission of John the Baptist? See Luke 1:17

9) In what ways would the beast out of the earth accomplish his goals?
[See 2 Thessalonians 2:9-12]

10) In what ways did John the Baptist accomplish his goals?
See Luke 3:16, John 10:41

Discussion:

The beast out of the earth was given great latitude and power (vv. 13-15) that was not given to John the Baptist. Why do you think God withheld miraculous powers from John but granted such power to one so evil?

11) Six is the number of man. When did this number originate? See Genesis 1:27-31

The number six is one short of Scripture's number seven which represents perfection. This study takes the position that 666 represents evil's unholy trinity and the counterpart to the Holy Trinity. (Revelation 1:4-5) Therefore, the beast out of the earth is the counter part to the Holy Spirit. The Holy Spirit came from above, the unholy spirit comes from below. We should not be too dogmatic and not consider a designated individual such as head of an Apostate Church as Satan's representative in the world. Satan has always been in the church business and he has been cunning enough to select religions that have global influence on millions of unsuspecting souls. Revelation chapters seventeen through nineteen examines this subject.

12) Verse eighteen calls for the wisdom of Jeremiah 17:5. Write down Jeremiah 17:5

Summary Statement:

Chapter one introduced the Holy Trinity. (Rev. 1:4) Chapter thirteen introduces the unholy trinity. (Satan/dragon – antichrist/beast from the sea – unholy spirit/beast from the earth)

Leader's Helicopter Overview for Revelation 13
(Optional or Prepare Your Own)

Is the _"man of lawlessness"_ (antichrist) a real person or is he merely a concept? _"Don't let anyone deceive you in any way, for the day of the Lord will not come until the man of lawlessness is revealed. He will oppose and will exalt himself over everything that is called God or is worshiped, so that he sets himself up in God's Temple, proclaiming himself to be God."_ (2 Thessalonians 2:2-3) Paul is not given to imagery so surely we can safely say antichrist is a real person! Many believe Jesus provided additional insight to antichrist being a real person. And further, the Temple in Jerusalem is going to be rebuilt! (Matthew 24:15) What do you think?

Daniel 9:27 confirms antichirst as a person rather than a concept? Concepts don't make agreements, people do! _"He will confirm a covenant with many for one seven._ (7 yrs.) _In the middle of the seven he will put an end to sacrifice and offering. And on a wing of the Temple, he will set up an abomination_ (idol) _that causes desolation, until the end that is decreed is poured out on him."_ He is used four times so we are speaking of an individual, not a concept! The idol antichrist sets up is most likely a picture of himself but it could be a military coat of arms.

Who antichrist is, is the subject many books are written and many political lies are suggested. What better way to discredit a political opponent than to spin the idea he is the antichrist! In this sense consider this verse, _"they will gather around them a great number of teachers who say what their itching ears want to hear. They will turn their ears away from the truth and turn aside to myths."_ (2 Timothy 4:3-4)

Daniel 12:36-39 might suggest antichrist to be a Jew or have Jewish linage. Further speculation suggests an ancestry linking back to the tribe of Dan. That he will come from the area of the Danube River in Europe. This has credibility because the tribe of Dan migrated north and is omitted from the sealed tribes of Israel. (Revelation 7) Some suggest him being homosexual (Daniel 12:37) depending on the Bible you read. Be careful, this verse could also have other meanings as some suggest, including the desire of Jewish women wishing to give birth to the Messiah.

For sure, antichrist will be the consummate liar and betrayer in the line of Judas. For as Judas, antichrist will appear to be something he isn't! (Revelation 6:2)

Application

*Do you see the frightening truth Judas demonstrates? Yes, it is possible to be in intimate gatherings with Christ, hear His teaching, and see His power before our very eyes, and be lost! Only at our invitation can Christ surgically open the blocked artery that connects the head to the heart. Beth Moore

*Living Beyond Yourself – Beth Moore - Copyright 1998 Reprinted and used by Permission of - Life Way Press ISBN 0-6331-93811-1

v. 1	dragon	Satan
v. 1	sea	the nations - world system (Isaiah 57:20)
v. 1	beast from the sea	antichrist - man of lawlessness
v. 1	horns - heads/crowns	federation of godless governments - readings in Daniel suggest a revived Roman Empire
v. 2	leopard	suggests menacing swiftness (Daniel 7:5)
v. 2	bear	suggests ferocious strength (Daniel 7:5)
v. 2	lion	suggests fierce overwhelming power (Daniel 7:4)
v. 3	wound was healed	new life to what was thought to be mortally wounded
v. 5	forty-two months	*"time of Jacob's trouble"* (Jeremiah 30:7)
v. 7	saints	not the Church (1 Thessalonians 4:17) these are Tribulation saints
v. 9	has an ear	mankind is divided, not by election here, but by freewill
v. 10	captivity	those who choose the mark of the beast
v. 10	sword	those who choose Christ can anticipate being martyred
v. 11	beast from the earth	spirit from below - opposite from Spirit from above - some believe to be a single individual or perhaps more than one
v. 12	fatal wound healed	either a manmade deception or a God ordained delusion
v. 13	great signs - wonders	whatever this is, delusional people buy into it
v. 14	an image	this will take place in Jerusalem at the Temple (Daniel 10:35, 11:31, Matthew 24:15)
v. 16	mark	accepts antichrist so as to be able to sustain the good life
v. 17	buy - sell	license to engage daily commerce – sustain earthly pleasures
v. 18	666	man's number (Genesis 1:27-31) blotted out of the book of life
v. 18	wisdom	risk standing alone, reject legalism, embrace Christ alone

Notes for Revelation 13

REVELATION 14
The Lamb, Israel and a Parade of Angels

This chapter seemingly is a break from the action but this is not the case. It is simply a break from a description of the Judgments. Judgments that are the fulfilling of prophecy. Here, John is describing these activities. Keep in mind, the Judgments themselves are ongoing for seven consecutive years.

Read Revelation 14:1-5

1) What does the term *"first fruits"* in relation to the 144,000 represent? See Romans 13:25-26

Discussion:

Does the illustration of the 144,000 not being defiled by women lead you to believe there are no women among the group being redeemed? How would you explain this to another person?

2) What does Genesis say about man and woman? See Genesis 2:15-18

Read Revelation 14:6-13

3) a. What is the message of the first angel? See Glossary, Ecclesiastes 12:13

   b. How is the Eternal Gospel different from the Gospel of Christ?

4) Is the 144,000 identified here the same 144,000 in chapter seven? Explain your answer!

5) What do you think *"a new song"* represents? See Glossary

6) In spite of the mass deaths and destruction of the Tribulation, many will be chosen to dwell on earth for the Millennial Kingdom. What does Jesus say about who these people will be? See Matthew 25:31-46

7) What is the message of the second angel? See Glossary

8) What is the warning of the third angel?

9) What does the third angel promise for those who take the mark of the beast?

10) What is the promise for those who persevere in their love for Jesus?

11) What does the Spirit of God promise the Tribulation saints? See Revelation 22:12

Read Revelation 14:14-20

12) What does fire from the alter represent? See Revelation 8:3

13) How are the three angels in verses fifteen through twenty different from the first three angels?

14) How is the harvest here different from how we generally view harvest?

Summary Statement:

Long rejected as their Messiah, Jesus gathers with the *"first fruits"* of Israel! Jesus is coming through the front door with busloads of His people with Him! The old tenants are being systematically ejected out the back door where *"all the birds are filled with their flesh."* (Revelation 19:21)

Let us not misidentify the 144,000. These are the same 144,000 Jews sealed in chapter seven. *"They sang a new song"* connects them to God's covenant people! (Exodus 15:1) *"Who had been redeemed from the earth"* (v. 3) is conveniently misinterpreted by some religious sects who brazenly identify themselves as the chosen 144,000! *"From the earth"* simply means God gathers His covenant people from the four corners of the earth. Since David, Zion is connected to Israel!

Are only men to be redeemed from Israel? John does seem to say in verse four that we are speaking of men only when he writes of them not being defiled by women. This being so, men only shall be the first fruits of a redeemed Israel. Assuredly ladies, just as Adam came first, Eve followed! Apparently, women will follow the 144,000 men! Certainly God blessed both equally! *"God created man in His own image, in the image of God He created him; male and female He created them. God blessed them and said to them, fill the earth."* (Genesis 1:27-28)

Some might say a man must be celibate to be one of the 144,000. That would suggest a wife defiles her husband? Folks, that is the deception of legalistic nonsense. *"For it is by grace, you have been saved, through faith, and this not from yourselves, it is the gift of God, not by any work"* (Ephesians 2:8) When Jesus spoke from the cross *"It is finished"* He meant just that! (John 19:30) This study takes the position that the point John makes here is these 144,000 men were simply not promiscuous either before or during marriage. It is true, the Tribulation period is not a good time to marry and bring children into the world! But to suggest a wife defiles her husband is a stretch! See Glossary

The first three angels are messenger angels to the people of the earth. They warn but take no punitive action. The next angel (v. 19) is a messenger to Christ who is holding *"a sharp sickle in this hand."* (v. 14) A fifth angel with *"a sharp sickle"* appears followed by a sixth angel who has charge of the fires of Judgment. He signals the fifth angel to avenge those who were murdered for their testimony. (Revelation 6:9) At this point, the prayers of the Tribulation martyrs and perhaps martyrs of all generations are answered! (Revelation 6:10)

If this were a movie, what follows you would not allow your children to view! We can surmise earthquakes reshaped Palestine so that John's description of blood rising as high as a horse's bridle is not too farfetched!

Application
Rest on verse thirteen! Until then, live a life abiding in Him. Maranatha!

Glossary of Imagery by Verse for Revelation 14

v. 1	Lamb	Christ
v. 1	Mt. Zion	location Christ will govern for the Millennium (Jerusalem)
v. 2	rushing water – thunder	voice of authority
v. 3	a new song	great anticipation of deliverance (Exodus 15:1)
v. 3	living creatures	see glossary in Revelation 4:6
v. 4	undefiled by women	metaphor for men of integrity
v. 4	first fruits	represents first step for the redemption of Israel (Romans 13:25-26)
v. 6	Everlasting Gospel	*"Revere God and give Him glory"* in the coming Millennium
v. 8	Babylon	the world system
v. 8	adulteries	not sexual as in human understanding of the word - Biblically this has to do with unfaithfulness to God, meaning man has greater love for materialism than for Jesus
v. 9	beast	antichrist
v. 9	mark	666 or any mark that identifies one with the world system
v. 12	saints	here it is people of the Great Tribulation who are faithful to Jesus
v. 14	sickle	life ending Judgment
v. 15	harvest	death of the ungodly
v. 19	winepress	plain and simple, the bloodbath of Armageddon (Revelation 16:16)
v. 20	outside city	God will not allow the forces coming against Zion to be successful
v. 20	stadia	from the Greek word for stadium - roughly two hundred miles or the length of Palestine from north to south... ....

Notes for Revelation 14

REVELATION 15 – 16
Seven Bowl Judgments

Chapter fifteen is a prelude to chapter sixteen and so we combine the two. John describes the opening of the law God gave Moses at Mr. Sinai who in turn made them known on earth. The nations, that is, the people of the earth have been found guilty of breaking God's law and have come under Judgment. Seven angels are the executioners!

Read Revelation 15
1) Identify the people in verse two and explain your conclusion. See Revelation 13:14-18

<u>Read Revelation 16</u>
2) Identify the targets of each of the seven angel's Judgments and comment on what the effects would inflict.

     a. First angel: target?
                                     result?

     b. Second angel: target?
                                       result?

     c. Third angel: target?
                                       result?

     d. Fourth angel: target?
                                       result?

     e. Fifth angel: target?
                                       result?

f.　Sixth angel:　　　　　target?

　　　　　　　　　　　　　　result?

　　g.　Seventh angel:　　　　target?

　　　　　　　　　　　　　　result?

3)　What is the mission of the three evil spirits?

4)　Identify who is responding in verse 16:7 and why they would be responding.
　　See Revelation 6:9-10

5)　What was the response of those who had never loved the Lord? (vv. 16:9, 11)

6)　Who is speaking in verse 16:15? See 1 Thessalonians 5:2

7)　With the aid of a Bible dictionary, explain Armageddon, what it represents and suggest the location geographically in relation to Jerusalem.

Discussion:
Name the sources of the unholy trinity in verse 16:13. Why do you think there is no mention of even one nation identified as being a defender on the side of God or His covenant people, Israel?

Summary Statement:
If it hadn't been clear before, it is clear now. No one can good their way out of God's Judgment! Or are there enough Sunday mornings for a person to attend a church enough to escape the Wrath of God! For if good works and/or church attendance were sufficient, people would have no need of God's Mercy in Christ.

We see a uniting of the Old Testament and the New Testament with joint singing the song of Moses and the Lamb. (vv. 3-4) It is encouraging to read in chapter 15:2-4 that in spite of severe testing in regard to being tempted to take the mark of the beast, (Chapter 13) people have come to the Lord. They are in heaven and are about the business of praising God! The reference to such terms as Tabernacle, Temple and plagues makes it perfectly clear, God is protecting Israel here and not the Church. As stated in earlier lessons, the last we see of the Church was in chapter three. She reappears later in chapter nineteen, not as a Church but as a Bride. To insist the Church will suffer the Great Tribulation is just wrong as documented in earlier lessons. See Zechariah 14:5 A reading of Zechariah 14 is recommended.

Discussion:
Concerning the Tribulation saints, some say they are those who had not heard the Gospel of Christ before the removal of the Church (1 Thessalonians 4:15-18, Revelation 3:10) but have responded to the message of the 144,000 (Revelation 7) or the two witnesses. (Revelation 11) Perhaps also, Tribulation saints include believers who were left behind at the Rapture because they were not born-again believers, carnal Christians if you will. However, some believe if a person had heard the message of the Gospel of Christ and rejected it, they are without hope once the removal of the Church has taken place. What do you think and is there Scripture supporting your thinking?

Application

Many a good person will go to hell! Lots of them. [See Matthew 7:13-14] Regardless of how benign their wrong-doings or even how much they benefited humanity, they will be judged against the perfection of the Law. The First Commandment alone will doom all who lived apart from God. As for the rest of the Commandments, to the last man <u>all will be found wanting and that is why we need Christ</u>! *"For all have sinned and fallen short of the glory of God"* (Romans 3:23)

Understanding Sin from God's Perspective!

We connect evil to Hitler, murderers, swindlers, thieves and pedophile predators. But <u>God, being the Maker of all things views all who live apart from Him as rebellious</u>! *"I, the Lord your God, am a jealous God."* (Exodus 20:5) Living apart from Him translates into a lethal mindset of *'I don't need God'* which puts emphasis on self! Self-thinking is viewed by our Lord as prideful rebellion! It is God who gave man life and the skills to live in the world that He, not man, created! (Genesis 2:8-15) Not one person will live in the Millennial Kingdom who doesn't accept this truth. For all who live in the coming Millennium will live by the Eternal Gospel. "Revere *God and give to Him all glory!"* (Revelation 14:6-7)

Chapter 15

v. 1	last plagues	plagues were instrumental to discipline Israel (Leviticus 26:25) to free the Jews in Egypt (Exodus 8-11) now to free God's people from the evil works of the unholy trinity at work in the nations
v. 2	sea of glass mixed with fire	description of the misery crushed up glass and fire would cause if one had to swim in it – represents what Tribulation saints endured for not having taken the mark of the beast
v. 3	song of Moses - Lamb	a singing celebration of those whom God redeemed in both the Old Testament and New Testament
v. 5	Temple – Tabernacle - Testimony	Old Testament dwelling place of God
v. 7	bowls	Wrath of God
v. 8	smoke	Old Testament symbol of God's glory (Exodus 19:16-18, 40:34-35)

Chapter 16

v. 3	sea	sea normally is the symbol for nations - here it refers to the oceans
v. 8	sun will scorch	ozone compromised - melting glaciers raise ocean levels and obliterate seaports and coastal cities - crops die
v. 10	darkness	not a loss of sunlight, but a loss of civil law - Societal darkness engulfs the world
v. 13	three evil spirits	exert their influence on governmental leaders
v. 13	unholy trinity	dragon is Satan - first beast is antichrist (Revelation 13:1) second beast is the false prophet or the apostate church (Revelation 13:11)
v. 14	signs	deceptions designed to motivate governments to invade Palestine (Psalm 2:1-5, Joel 3:1-2)
v. 16	Armageddon	Apocalyptic struggle - good vs. evil. See 2 Thessalonians 1:7-10 and (Revelation 14:20, Joel 2:11)
v. 17	seventh bowl	final judgment of Daniel's seventieth week
v. 19	great city	only city mentioned in relation to Christ's Kingdom is Jerusalem
v. 19	three part split	Mount of Olives split in two parts with a valley in between (Zechariah 14:4) For additional details of the Kingdom See Zechariah 14
v. 19	Babylon	world system and its cities reduced to dust - remembered no more

REVELATION 17
The Church that is Not

Within the apostate church, the issue is not the absence of a moral code, it is the absence of saving truth! All religions embrace a moral code, but not all religions embrace Salvation through Christ alone. *"Salvation is found in no one else, for there is no other name under heaven given to men by which we must be saved."* (Acts 4:12) <u>Without Jesus, no church has a message worth turning on the lights.</u> Unfortunately, by the edicts of officials, some religious institutions assign its people additional requirements. When this occurs, the power of the cross is watered down! Revelation seventeen is an indictment of such practices. This chapter examines the apostate church and antichrist's use of it in the seven year Tribulation. (Daniel's seventieth week) The greatest danger of the apostate church is that it resembles the real thing!

The apostate church will send more people to hell than the opinions of a thousand Atheists!

Read Romans 3:21-4:6

1) Where does righteousness come from?

2) Who would be glorified if works saved a man?

3) a. Is there anything in Romans 3:21-4:6 that indicate in addition to Christ, a Church should add additional requirements for Salvation?

   b. Write the three Last Words of Jesus. See John 19:30

4) What is legalism and what are its dangers?

5) a. Did good works make Abraham a righteous man or was it something else?

   b. Write Romans 4:3

   c. Write Genesis 15:6

   d. Are there other ways to heaven other than Christ alone such as abiding by rules, working at a church or singing in the choir etc.?

   In short, can you work or good your way to heaven? _____

6) a. Using a Bible dictionary, define Grace.

   b. What was God's provision for the redemption of sin? See John 3:16

7) Any religious or church body that is founded by anyone other than Jesus Christ is called a _ _ _ t.

Discussion:
What are some false teachings of cult churches?

Read Revelation 17:1-5
8) What is the relationship between the woman and governments? (v.2)

9) Antichrist will use a <u>worldwide religious order</u> to leverage the masses. Using the forensics of verses three and four, what world religions might qualify?

Discussion:
What are the ramifications of a political party identifying itself with the Church?

Name some nations where government and religion are joined at the hip. What has been the result of this marriage?

Read Revelation 17:6-11
10) Why do you think some would be joyful at witnessing the execution of God's people? See Revelation 11:7-10

Read Revelation 17:12-18
11) There are many examples of God working through good men and women to accomplish His purpose. But what does verse seventeen tell you about God working through evil people to accomplish His purpose?

Summary Statement:
This chapter is a wakeup call to be wary of those who would use the Church or any religious institution to elevate their image. *"This calls for wisdom"* (Revelation 13:18)

Apostate institutions cover the earth. Of course <u>antichrist will align himself with the strongest among them to control the masses</u>. The same can be said for the media. That will be addressed in the next chapter. After antichrist uses the apostate institutions to accomplish his mission, he will turn against it and destroy it which is exactly how God planned! (Revelation 17:16-17)

This chapter is a call to not be asleep at the wheel spiritually! To be blunt, stupid! *"The man without the Spirit does not accept the things that come from the Spirit of God for they are foolishness to him and he cannot understand them, because they are spiritually discerned."* (1 Corinthians 2:14) Those who are spiritually unaware are vulnerable to the devil's deceptions, principally, false teaching.

This chapter is a throw-back to chapters two and three in regard to institutions of worship. It is the Bible's last heads up concerning an awareness there are apostate religious institutions in the world. Perhaps there is even one in your community. Or worse, you are attending one. There is nothing more reproachful than to be a part of something called a harlot! (Revelation 17:16)

There are more flavors of doctrine than there are flavors of ice cream. And they can't all be right! So how do we separate the true Church from the apostate church? Go to the source, <u>the Word of God</u>, not the writings of a founder not named Jesus. Romans chapters one through eight is the hallmark of Christianity that correctly states the Good News of Jesus Christ as illustrated in the Gospels. <u>It is the intent of this study to structure each lesson to the Word of God</u> without regard for the doctrines of religious institutions. *"For if we are trying to please men, we would not be servants of God."*

None of us should feel obligated to an institution for our salvation. It is Christ who died for you and He is to be your focus. (Revelations 2:4) Babylon is an amalgamation of remaining isms after true believers are taken up. (2 Thessalonians 4:16-17, Revelation 3:10) This question, who today is on track with being the Bride and who is on track with being the harlot? You need to know this! Revelation 3:7-22 reveals the answer. The Church at Philadelphia and the Church at Laodicea.

Application

Institutions are not saved, people are! Therefore, let us not allow our place of worship to lead us down the path to condemnation through errant teachings.

Review Revelation 2 Overview and Application: Revelation 3 Application.

Glossary of Imagery by Verse for Revelation 17

v. 1	great prostitute	unfaithfulness - not sexual but since the tower of Babel and Nimrod, humankind has been a promiscuous worshiping pimp parading a laundry list of gods before the Creator - God's personal visit in the person of Jesus Christ has separated the faithful from the unfaithful.
v. 1	many waters	global
v. 2	adultery	again not sexual - world leaders view antichrist the world authority
v. 2	inhabitants	society also views antichrist as the authority in their lives
v. 3	desert	a godless place that is the residence of the apostate church
v. 3	woman	not the same woman in chapter twelve - this is the woman in verse one
v. 3	scarlet beast	scarlet is associated with a prominent world religious order - beast is antichrist who uses this world religion to leverage the masses -Some try to explain away scarlet using Exodus 25:3 and Exodus 26. The problem with that theory is, it is highly unlikely Judaism will be Global. In fact, just the opposite, anti-Semitism will be global. For that reason, this study cannot correlate this woman with Israel
v. 3	seven heads - ten horns	power centers of the world - could be governments, media or both
v. 4	purple	Roman imperialism of John's time - every senator and consul was identified by this color
v. 4	scarlet	represents adopted color of a world religion
v. 4	adorned	by pomp or other means, harlot makes herself appealing to the masses.
v. 4	golden cup	harlot's wealth
v. 5	forehead	Roman prostitutes were identified by headbands in John's day
v. 5	Babylon - Mother of Prostitutes...	This is an amalgamation of religious error inclusive of some Protestants, Cults and all sects that end with ism! All can be tied to the Church at Laodicea. (Revelation 3) This is what is left after the true Church is removed. (1 Thessalonians 4:16-17, Revelation 3:10) The antichrist will use one or all of these religious sects until the time of betrayal (Revelation 17:16)
v. 8	was - is not – now is	a revived Roman Empire or perhaps antichrist apparent deceptive death and resurrection (Revelation 13:3-4)
v. 9	seven hills	Rome sits on seven hills - may refer to the seven powers
v. 14	make war	Armageddon
v. 16	leave her	When antichrist has achieved his desired position, he will discard anything resembling an institution of religion. For even an errant religious institution has a code of conduct which he will oppose.
v. 18	great city	not Jerusalem, but Babylon which is representative of a world full of unfaithfulness and apostate harlotry... ...

REVELATION 18
Where Are You Invested?

You and I are chronological creatures and like things presented to us in that order. If we haven't already figured it out, the chapters are not chronological. The Book of Revelation is well suited to view sitting in a theater surrounded by seven screens. Instead of sitting on a fixed seat facing one direction, you sit on a swivel seat viewing <u>a panorama of events all related to one unfolding theme.</u>

For example, the narrative here is almost certain aligned with the fifth bowl judgment (Revelation 16:10) and verse four *"Come out of her my people"* is aligned with the beast. (Revelation 13) Also, Jesus' Words *"Do not store up for yourselves treasures on earth"* (Matthew 6:19) has a certain relevance to the narrative here. This chapter contains heaven's last warning (v. 4) for people to not invest in the culture of Babylon! Specifically, don't take the mark of 666 which represents business as usual.

1) <u>From the list below, what attracts you more to attend a religious service?</u>

   The Music _____ The pomp and circumstance of a colorful service _____

   The oratory skills of the preacher _____ Love for the Lord and His Word _____

   The Large campus _____ Youth Programs _____ Social Network _____

2) <u>Which is less offensive to God to steal from or cheat?</u>

   The IRS _____ a Large Corporation _____ Insurance Company _____

   a Bank _____ a stranger _____ a Friend _____ all would be equally sinful _____

Read Revelation 18:1-8
1) What is verse four in reference to? See Revelation 13:15-18

2) The culture of the world system is referred to in the feminine gender. How does verse seven describe the character of the secular culture of earth?

3) How quick and complete will God's Judgment be when it comes? (v. 8)

Read Revelation 18:9-19
4) The catastrophe that comes upon the earth will include loss other than life.

   a. What are some things affluent people will lose?

   b. What are some things people with little means will lose?

Discussion:

If Christ removed His Church and you were left behind, how would you adjust your mind so as to remove the temptation to take the mark of the beast when it comes?

5) People under Judgment include affluent people and people of little means. What one thing do both have in common?

6) What is the fate of one who rejects the Son of God? See Revelation 20:15

7) What is the lament of men who make their living from the sea?

8) Who are the people vindicated by the catastrophes on earth?
See Revelation 6:9-11

Read Revelation 18:20-24

9) What are the emotions recorded here of those who are in heaven?

Discussion:

Are the emotions of the heavenly hosts, emotions you would identify with?

Author's Note:

Even through the Ecclesiastical and commercial collapse, there still remains a massive army to come against Jerusalem. The seventh angel (Revelation 16:17-21) initiates the final blow that Christ will complete in chapter nineteen. Chapter 16:17-21 connects to Chapter 19:11-21.

Summary Statement:

One would think God would be the One to destroy Ecclesiastical Babylon, but He uses commercial Babylon to do the job for Him. (Revelation 17:16-17)

We are at a time coastal cities have fallen into the sea and inland cities are dust along with much of the world population. Nothing resembling the work of man remains as God prepares the way for a new order. What will replace what man has built is anybody's guess. We can be sure it will be wonderful! Those who are a part of the Kingdom of God will live by *"the Eternal Gospel."* (Revelation 14:6) In our cosmic journey, the choices we make are irrevocable!

How wonderful our God is to let us see the future. Men will have no excuse for investing their life poorly! Who in their right mind would have invested in Enron had they seen that it was destined to collapse? Yet many do so every day. In verse four, God calls on people to not invest in an institution (earth) destined to collapse!

<u>Let nothing detract from the Lord Jesus.</u> (v. 4) Do not invest in religious pomp because the allure of flowing robes, sashes and gold trim are so compelling; Or religions identified by turbans, head rubies (Revelation 17:4) or even the portfolios of Wall Street. None of this is going to heaven! Roman Catholicism, Hinduism, Buddhism, Islam, Mormonism, Denominationalism and the laundry lists of Karmas are not going to heaven! All are absent in Scripture and all will be absent in heaven. Like the Pharisee crowd of Jesus' day, the Lord detests showboat religion! He has not prepared a place for them. If you are invested in religious panache or the culture of commercialism and its subsequent pleasures of the flesh, beloved you are in grave danger.

Author's Note: It is not the intent of this study to discredit the institutional church. But rather, to keep us mindful <u>it is the Blood of the Lamb that assures one's Salvation</u> and not the institutional church, its leaders or its edicts. The institutional church is not written in the Book of Life and will not be in heaven, people will. Certainly large bodies require governing and we acknowledge such, as governing was established in Jerusalem in the First Century by the Apostles.

Verse four calls people to a <u>life change before time runs out</u>! Change begins at home. The home is where character forms that spills out into the culture. <u>Change starts with one's relationship with God</u>! Assembling together for worship is obligatory for a Christian! Daily prayer and Bible study is a must! Being a loophole society, people easily rationalize away God's Commands through the use of loophole excuses.

After God, relationship with both father and mother follows and is a Commandment! But some believers seek loopholes to avoid this Command. They do all the right Christian things but rationalize disenfranchising one or both parents. Christ calls such people hypocrites. (Matthew 15:3-9) <u>Money or service they give to the Church is corban and an affront to the Spirit of Love</u>. (Mark 7:11) In efforts to deceive others of their holiness, they deceive themselves. Paul writes they are worse than unbelievers. (1 Tim. 5:8) Spouses who endeavor to demean a mate in the eyes of children unwittingly plant seeds of lifelong sin in their children who as adults, dishonor the targeted parent. From the home to the justice system to government, loopholes are a way of life and the product of earthen culture. Beloved, loopholes are the devils noose!

<u>Application</u>
For where your treasure is, there your heart will be also." (Matthew 6:19-21)

Glossary of Imagery by Verse for Revelation 18

v. 1	another angel	apparently a companion angel to the fifth bowl angel (Revelation 16:10) his role is to make a proclamation rather than the pouring out of Wrath
v. 2	fallen - Babylon	not an announcement of the Judgment completed, rather an announcement about how low humankind had sunk *"She has become"* has to do with humankind's condition
v. 3	adulteries	has to do with spiritual unfaithfulness
v. 4	another voice	Seemingly is another opportunity to repent. This is the last one.
v. 7	widow	a boastful culture that has never been defeated (until now!)
v. 9	weep - mourn	realization what the world loves, $$, lust, pleasure, power is no more
v. 17	one hour	when Judgment comes, its final hour will be swift
v. 18	great city	again, not a specific city but all earthen centers of commerce
v. 21	millstone	metaphor for a cataclysmic end of earth as we know it
v. 23	Bridegroom - Bride	A second rebellion will occur at the end of the Millennial Kingdom where Gog and Magog will come against Christ and His Bride. (See Revelation 20:7-9)
v. 24	blood	Since Cain slew Able, godly men and women have been murdered. The sentence for murder is death to a culture of evil.

Notes for Revelation 18

Accessing the Scriptures

REVELATION 19
King of Kings, Lord of Lords

The Second Coming of Jesus Christ is the theme of this chapter. The result anticipated, *"sinners vanish from the earth and the wicked be no more."* (Psalm 104:35) This is the chapter that everyone who loves the Lord Jesus anticipates. Hallelujah!

Read Revelation 19:1-10

1) Describe the emotions of the multitude who are in heaven.

2) What does the heavenly multitude say about God's Judgment?

Discussion:

Earth as we know it lies in ruble. Hotels and restaurants you have enjoyed are gone. If you had unbelieving friends and family, all will be absent from the earth. This is the reality of the return of the Gentle Carpenter from Nazareth. What do you think about all of this and what will you look forward to?

3) Where there is a bride, there also is a groom. Who does the following Scriptures identify as the Bride and Groom?

    a. See 2 Corinthians 11:2, Ephesians 5:22-29

    b. See John 3:28-29

4) In earthen culture, what things must a bride do to make herself appear beautifully adorned at her wedding?

5) What did Christ do for His Bride to make her radiant that she wasn't able to do for herself? See Ephesians 5:25-27

6) What nation of people will be among the guests at the Wedding Supper of the Lamb? See Matthew 8:11

7) Where is the Wedding Feast to be held? See Matthew 8:11-12, Revelation 5:10

8) What happens to the Bride prior to coming back to earth? See 2 Corinthians 5:10

Read Revelation 19:11-16

9) Scripture describes four arrival and departure events. Christians must be clear on them and generally able to locate them in the Bible: Identify the event taking place.

    a. Matthew 1:18-25

    b. Acts 1:9-11

    c. 1 Thessalonians 4:13-17

    d. Revelation 19:11-16

10) Compare the Rider on the white horse in this chapter with the rider on the white horse in Revelation 6:2

11) Who is the angel calling to and for what purpose is he calling to them?

12) What is the fate of antichrist and the false prophet? (v. 20)

13) The army against the Lord *"were killed by the sword."* Certainly, not by a steel sword! So what killed them? See Genesis 1:3, 6, 9, 11, 14, 20, 24

Summary Statement:

In the eternal state, no lines are drawn. But in this chapter we are in the Kingdom state and lines of distinction exist. The Bride here is the Church. Certainly a bride isn't a guest at her own wedding. Other than angels, that leaves the guests to be Old Testament saints, Tribulation saints and the Redeemed of Israel.

The Rider on the white horse is Christ. He came to earth the first time as a Lamb and His Second Coming is that of a Lion! Interestingly, Satan is not the first being cast into the lake of fire. (Revelation 20:10) Antichrist and the false prophet are the first to be cast into the lake of fire. Satan and the sum total of all unbelievers will join them in one thousand years. (Revelation (20:15)

The appearance of Christ here is not the same as 1 Thessalonians 4:15-17. In that event, Christ remains in the air as He removes the Church from the earth thus sparing Her the coming Wrath. Only His Own will see Him at that event. It would be seven more years (Revelation 19) before Christ literally comes down to earth and <u>every eye shall see Him</u>. (Revelation 1:7) This is the Second Coming!

This chapter is the fulfillment of too many prophecies to name them all. The biggest is Christ's Second Coming. Other fulfillments are; God delivers Israel, reappearance of the Church as the Bride, Divine Justice completed, enemies of God crushed, God's Sovereignty fully orchestrated, God establishes communion with His people, the world system is replaced as Jesus reigns as King of Kings and Lord of Lords!

"Let the sinners vanish from the earth, and the wicked be no more. Praise the Lord O' my soul, Praise the Lord." (Psalm 104:35) This Psalm identifies two kinds of people, sinners and truly evil people. <u>From God's perspective, all men are sinners</u>. *"For all have sinned and fallen short of the glory of God."* (Romans 3:23) By His Grace, God provided a Righteousness in the sacrifice of His Son for all who would receive Him. <u>Anyone who refused Christ was an affront to the Mercy of God</u>! In God's economy, that person is rebellious and prideful. Choosing to trust in their own works, God will grant them their wish! (Revelation 20:12)

Jesus rode into Jerusalem on a donkey, the humblest of animals. His return is on a white stallion, an animal for a King at war. He is called Faithful because the things He promised to His covenant people, the Church and yes, even to His enemies have come to pass! He is called True for He is Inherently Truth! At His crucifixion, thorns were placed on His head. Now multiple Crowns adorn His head indicating the magnitude of His Kingdom.

<u>Application</u>
"The punishment that brought us peace was upon Him and by His wounds we are healed
"We all, like sheep, have gone astray, each of us to his own way"
"And the Lord has laid upon Him the iniquity of us all"
"He was led like a lamb to the slaughter"
"For He bore the sin of many, and made intercession for the transgressors"
(Isaiah 53)

Jesus came the first time to give Himself up for you! He comes the second time to engage His enemies. Where do you stand? Will you be with Him or you will be in the ground awaiting Judgment? (Revelation 20:12) *"Small is the gate and narrow the road that leads to life."* (Matthew 7:13) Beloved, plan wisely!

Glossary for Imagery by Verse for Revelation 19

v. 1	Hallelujah	appears four times in Scripture and only in this chapter
v. 1	multitude	heard but not seen - unidentified specifically – the concept of heaven's joy of the Sovereignty and Justice of God.
v. 4	twenty-four elders	see glossary for chapter 4
v. 4	four creatures	see glossary for chapter 4
v. 7	Bride	specifically the Church - some say Redeemed of all ages - to be consistent with itself, this study maintains the Church is the Bride (See Song of Songs 8:5)
v. 9	guests	redeemed out of the Tribulation - not a part of the Church the sheep living on earth (Matthew 25:31-46) the marriage takes place in heaven - the wedding banquet is an earthly event - other guests include angels and God's Covenant People, Israel - recall the 144,000, God's lieutenants to serve Him governing earth in the Millennium.
v. 11	heaven open	does not concern the Church coming to heaven - is about Jesus coming out of heaven to make war against His enemies
v. 11	White Horse	not the same white horse of chapter six - this is Christ! The white horse of chapter six was antichrist!
v. 12	eyes	nothing escapes the vision of Christ
v. 12	fire	this word is always connected with Judgment/Wrath
v. 13	blood	not blood from Armageddon which does not occur until verse fifteen. This is blood inclusive of all innocent blood shed from Abel who was slain by Cain to all righteous people murdered by unrighteous people of all generations. Certainly blood of all who ever opposed Satan and his forces.
v. 14	armies	Church, Old Testament saints, Tribulation saints and angels
v. 15	sharp sword	the power to make things happen are from the Mouth of God (Genesis 1:6, 9, 11, 14, 20, 24, 26, John 1:1)
v. 15	iron scepter	appears serval times in Scripture - first appeared in Psalm 2:9 Christ Kingdom on earth will be a theocracy
v. 15	winepress	Judgment
v. 16	King of Kings, Lord of Lords	stark contrast to Christ's first coming to earth
v. 17	supper	This is not a pretty sight and reason some refuse to study this book. But to limit God simply to Love would make Him unjust and diminish His Holiness.
v. 20	cast alive	Those who took the mark of the beast along with antichrist and his false prophet get a one thousand year head start entering the lake of fire. They are not a part of the White Throne Judgment (Revelation 20:11-15) because they will already be there… ….

REVELATION 20
"Thy Kingdom Come"

"Thy will be done, on earth." This chapter is the crown jewel for supporting the Premillennial (see overview) view of Christ's return and the Millennial Kingdom! Hence, our study takes a literal interpretation of the one thousand year Kingdom on earth. Amillennialism and Postmillennialism are introduced but this study makes no effort to give either credibility. Scripture is just not supportive of either. The literal Reign of Christ over earth will take place just as the prophets and Jesus Himself foretold.

Read Revelation 20:1-6

1) From the following passages, how did God use Satan?

   a. Job 1:8-12   b. Matthew 4:1-11

2) For what purpose do you think Satan *"must be released?"* (v. 3)

3) Identify some activities of the redeemed from both the Old Testament and New Testament? (v. 4) See Revelation 4:8-11

4) It has been demonstrated, God uses Satan to both test people and demonstrate the power of the Holy Spirit working in people's lives. Not the least of which was His Son? What does verse four suggest who will be tested during the one thousand years?

5) Where are the unredeemed from both Old and New Testament kept? (v. 5)

Discussion:

The age old question, why do you think God permits evil?

6) It may surprise some, but there are two resurrections. Identify the difference and how many years are they separated? For further insight see 1 Thessalonians 4:14-17

Read Revelation 20:7-10

7) So what is your answer why God releases Satan after one thousand years?

8) What does verses seven through nine suggest happens to *"Gog and Magog"* after one thousand years. Who are these players in God's plan for Creation?
   See Ezekiel 38:2, 18, 22, 39:1-9

Revelation 20:11-15

9) The fourth and final Judgment takes place in this section. It is important a student of Scripture be familiar with the four principal Judgments.

    a. What was judged in Luke 23:46? See Also 1 Peter 2:24

    b. Who is judged in 2 Corinthians 5:10?

    c. Who are judged in Matthew 25:31-46?

    d. Who are judged in Revelation 20:11-14?

Read Revelation 20:11-15

10) Judgment leaves nothing out. Identify what is judged in these passages.

    a. Luke 8:17

    b. Matthew 12:37

    c. Matthew 16:27

11) What is God's standard to judge? See Matthew 5:48, Leviticus 19:2

12) What will be discovered at this Judgment? See Romans 3:23

Discussion:

Why is it imperative to be with Christ?

13) What are the implications in the following verses of Matthew 11:22, Mark 12:38-40 and Luke 12:47-48?

Summary Statement:

Satan is chained for one thousand years making conditions on earth ideal. Mortals and immortals will co-exist. Immortals will reign with Jesus and extoll Him. After one thousand years Satan is released to test newly born mortals. Some will rebel and come against God and fire will rain down on them. Thereafter, the Second Resurrection takes place. These are the lost from both Old and New Testament. They are cast into the lake of fire which is called the second death forever and ever!

Leader's Helicopter Overview for Revelation 20
(Optional or Prepare Your Own)

This study takes the premillennial view of a literal reign of Jesus Christ over all the earth as foretold by the prophets. Immortals and mortals will coexist for one thousand years. Two other views are Amillennialism and Postmillennialism.

Amillennialism spiritualizes Christ's earthly reign. This view contends the Kingdom is symbolic only. But Amillennialism is riddled with difficulties, not the least of which is, how do we explain the resurrection of the dead? Secondly, this view fails to explain the second death or of the Church being caught-up. (1 Thessalonians 4:15-17)

Postmillennialism holds to the view the Church will Christianize the entire world, bringing peace for one thousand years and then Christ would come in peace, but this is so fraught with difficulties one does not know where to begin and so we won't.

This chapter is the pivotal point of what you believe about your faith! Do you take chapter 20 literally or symbolic of some heavenly euphoric state? Will you have a physical but altered body during the Millennium? The Resurrection of Jesus gives us insight. His appearance was physical and He physically occupied space. Further, the beatings and physical torture are not apparent to Mary Magdalene or others including Peter and the Twelve who were in contact with Him. Certainly the science of the resurrected body will be different but euphoric state is simply not what Jesus exhibited.

The obvious question one might ask, why does God release Satan again? Why not just get rid of him here? When you answer that question, then you will know why God permits evil. Of this J. Vernon McGee writes, 'tell me why God let him loose in the first place on the earth, I'll tell you why God lets him loose for a second time!' The mystery of God's program will one day be answered.

Satan's second release is additional evidence the Millennium will be a physical rather than a euphoric state. Satan's predatory domain is earthly. The Millennium will be a testing of the natural man under ideal conditions. We who are with Jesus will be unaffected by the release of Satan a second time.

Application

The Church was not designed to convert the world. It was designed to spread the Gospel to those who would listen! *"He who has an ear, let him hear."* Write down Jesus' promise in John 6:37

Glossary of Imagery by Verse for Revelation 20

v. 1	bottomless pit	same as the Abyss of Revelation 9:1 - This does not compute as the same place as hell. Evidently lost souls and demons are kept apart until the final Judgment. (White Throne Judgment)
v. 2	serpent	Satan
v. 2	thousand years	Millennial Kingdom on earth
v. 6	second death	spiritual death
v. 7	release Satan	See Overview
v. 8	Gog/Magog	Gog is a rebellious leader out of the earthly Millennial Kingdom. Magog is the name for his army of followers.
v. 9	beloved city	Jerusalem
v. 9	fire	Judgment
v. 10	deceived	a second Armageddon after one thousand years of peace.
v. 11	white throne	Judgment Seat of God without intercession - the place where those of the second resurrection (the lost v. 5) are judged - people who failed to take seriously John 6:28-29. They will stand on their own righteousness and will be found wanting.
v. 11	earth - sky fled away	several considerations - no where for sinners to hide - no mansions prepared for them (John 14:1-4) In a word, God speaks His first Creation out of existence. (2 Peter 3:1-13)
vv. 11-12	book - books	The Book of Life is singular. The lost require many books. *"Wide is the gate that leads to destruction."* Unlike the Redeemed who rest on John 6:28-29, the lost will stand on their own works that accompany their name.
v. 13	sea - death - hades	wherever sinners are located, they will not hide from justice... ....

Notes for Revelation 20

REVELATION 21
Paradise Regained

God's relationship with humans was lost in a garden. (Genesis 3) In mercy, God restores the relationship in a city that resembles a garden. This chapter is that place Jesus promised. *"I go to prepare a place for you, where I am you may also be with me"* (John 14:1-6)

Read Revelation 21:1-14

1) What do the words *"no more"* mean to you?

2) What does verse eight promise?

3) We have always heard it said that men cannot look at God and live. What is it that sets men apart that makes this so? See Romans 5:12, Isaiah 59:1-2

4) What has changed that you and I will be allowed to dwell with God? See Ephesians 2:18, Hebrews 10:19-23, 1 John 3:1-3

5) Why will there no longer be a need for door locks, alarm systems, police, gun manufacturing, tanks, bombs or a Secret Service? See Revelation 14:6-7

6) What happened in the Garden of Eden that led to the need of all the things listed in the previous question? See Genesis 3

7) Two covenant groups are identified in verses twelve through fourteen. What is the significance of each?

   a. Twelve Tribes of Israel/Gate

   b. Twelve Apostles/Foundation

   c. What does Ephesians 2:11-16 say about this union?

   d. Write down Galatians 3:26

8) How will New Jerusalem be different from today's Jerusalem? (v.11)

Discussion:
Verses twelve and fifteen describes the city surrounded by very high walls. Since we know the enemies of God are no longer on the scene to pose a threat to His people, explain why walls are present.

Read Revelation 21:15-21
9) How many precious stones decorate the Foundation walls of the city?

Read Revelation 21:22-27
10) Identify three things we see daily that the presence of the Lord will replace.

11) The Temple had always given the Jews a sense they alone possessed God but John writes that New Jerusalem will not have a Temple. Couple this with Jesus' words in John 2:19, what conclusion can we draw concerning the Jews and the Gentiles?

Time out: *"The first will be last and the last will be first"* (Matthew 19:30) is appropriate here. This significant verse lets us know there will be numerous surprises in regard to Redemption. One such surprise (there are several) is the eradication of the Jewish/Gentile culture of the early Church. It will be the Church that is redeemed before the chosen people. (1 Thessalonians 4:16-17)

12) Besides the New Jerusalem, describe God's glory appearing on the earth at other times.

   a. Exodus 40:34-38

   b. 2 Chronicles 7:1-3

   c. Matthew 17:1-8

Summary Statement:
This chapter provides a look at the size and architecture of New Jerusalem. Its proximity to earth is such that it is easily accessible to those who travel there. Those who longed to be with Jesus, God will grant them their wish. Those who didn't want any part of Jesus will get their wish also! What God had planned in the Garden of Eden is made manifest here.

The immediate challenge of this chapter is one of interpretation. Is this new earth literal or spiritual? If new earth is spiritual then why does David, Jesus and John all use the term earth? The use of much symbolism can get one so caught up they forget <u>what the Scriptures have taught</u>. *"The meek shall inherit the earth."* (Matthew 5:5) Do not listen to the skeptics, <u>listen to the Word of God</u>! *"It is trustworthy and true."* If we take both Old and New Testament as factual, why would we suddenly spiritualize this part of the Book of Revelation or its final two chapters? *"The meek shall inherit the earth and shall delight themselves in abundant peace."* (Psalm 37:11) Considering the Creation, is this so difficult?

<u>What we can anticipate is a science known only to God is now revealed</u>! Einstein said that the sum total of the knowledge of all men who ever lived is less than one tenth of one percent of total knowledge! What God has planned for His people is revealed in these final two chapters. A science where nothing decays or dies!

This would make the world of business if one exists not resemble the one today. Wonderfully, verse eight carries a message to John's readers that a time is coming when all inhabitants of the new earth will live by the Eternal Gospel, *"Fear God and give Him glory."* (Revelation 14:6) Imagine switching on the nightly news and not viewing man's inhumanity to man or observing snarky looking goons with crocodile looking assault rifles running amok in the streets of the world!

The specifics John gives us about the Holy City makes its size somewhat larger than the moon. Since all inhabitants will have twenty-four-seven access to the City we can conclude Jerusalem will be directly attached to the earth. The Boeing 737 will be replaced with a new travel science. Perhaps <u>telepathic relocation</u> is how people move about. Jesus, after His resurrection and others, demonstrated this in the Bible. With no sun, moon or night, we might assume the earth will no longer rotate or orbit.

Without consuming space with supporting Scriptures we will say the Church is at home in the Holy City with Jesus and the Jewish people have uncontested control of Israel. Governing responsibilities possibly are given to some to assist governing the Gentiles about the earth. These might be non-church Gentiles, Tribulation saints and or saints out of the Millennial Kingdom

Application

<u>Heaven is coming down to earth</u>. That is why when we pray *"Our Father who art in heaven, hallowed be Thy name, Thy Kingdom come, Your will be done, on earth as it is in heaven."* What God planned in the Garden of Eden is made manifest here. He will dwell with His people. Beloved, have you made plans to be a part of it?

Time out: *"Brothers, I do not want you to be ignorant about those who fall asleep. The dead in Christ will rise first. We who are alive will be caught-up with them."*

This excerpt from 1 Thessalonians coupled with the appearance of Elijah who never experienced physical death and Moses who did experience physical death tells us heaven is very real and not a state of euphoria. The citizens of the new earth just like now, will have need of nourishment and a place to obtain it. Much of this chapter and the next are an encouragement to John's readers who were living with barely enough to sustain them that a new day is coming when they will want for nothing. The glossary of the final two chapters reflects this concept.

Glossary of Imagery by Verse for Revelation 21

v. 1	new heaven - earth	A science known only to God will be revealed. A science where nothing decays or dies.
v. 1	sea	doesn't mean no more water - Sea has always represented a negative, from raging nations, storms, separation, a grave yard to the place figuratively, the beasts came from. (Revelation 13:1) Whatever water there is will be configured very differently.
v. 2	New Jerusalem	represents hope to John's readers then and now
v. 2	as a bride	present Jerusalem was rubble - this is the hope of the future
v. 6	water of life	God's provision - persevere
v. 7	overcomes	rejects the natural man and clothes himself with Christ
v. 8	fiery lake	sulfur defines its location is right under your feet
v. 9	Bride	Church (Song of Songs 8:5)
v. 12	high wall	not for keeping people out - represents Eternal Protection in Christ
v. 12	twelve gates	represents that it was through the Jewish people Christ came
v. 12	twelve foundations	represents it was through the Apostles the Church grew
v. 15	measuring rod	represents the care God went to in preparing for His people
v. 22	Temple	A reminder of the teachings of Jesus that He would replace the the bricks and mortar of a Temple made by human hands. This of course did not sit well with the Pharisees.
v. 24	"the nations will walk by its light"	People around the world, if the world is indeed round, will live by the Eternal Gospel. *"Fear God and give Him glory"* (Revelation. 14:6-7)

REVELATION 22
Water of Life and Epilogue

We move from the description of the eternal city to the <u>function of the city</u>. New Jerusalem will be a place of nourishment for inhabitants of the city, Israel and the nations. <u>What will be the perception you will take from John's final vision?</u> The prophecies of Jesus' birth, death, burial and resurrection were literally fulfilled. The Creation itself was literal. It makes no sense to spiritualize at this juncture. The new heavens and the new earth will be literal also? Yes, a new science will be revealed and at the center, God will be with His people, His original plan in the Garden of Eden.

Read Revelation 22:1-6

1) What are some of the misconceptions people believe about Eternal Life?

2) If no human was around when God established the Creation, on what basis do you think nay-sayers stand on concerning creation?

3) a. On what do you base your belief that heaven and hell both exist?

    b. Write down Romans 4:3.

4) Compare the tree in Revelation 22:2 with the tree in Genesis 2:1

5) What are the implications of verses one and two of this chapter?

6) What do the following verses say about seeing God face to face?

    a. Exodus 33:20

    b. 1 Timothy 6:14-16

    c. Revelation 22:3-4

    d. Psalm 11:7

    e. Matthew 5:8

Time out: There are accounts in scripture that might appear contradictory to the casual reader. No mortal man has seen the face of God (John 1:18) yet Numbers 12:6-8 and Deuteronomy 34:10 say otherwise. Be aware, the Bible like most books, incorporate various <u>literary devices to make a point</u>. *'Face to face'* is used to have us understand God's direct table talk conversations with Moses, not eye to eye contact. Another and more troubling example is Jesus' use of hyperbole to make His point about what position He is to be in a person's life when He said *"If anyone does not hate his father and mother, his wife and children, his brothers and sisters – yes, even his own life – he cannot be my disciple."* (Luke 14:26) It is always good to have a Study Bible available when encountering troubling verses.

Read Revelation 22:7-21

7) What mistake did John make that he had already made in Revelation 19:9-10?

8) How does the angel identify himself? (v. 9)

9) Compare John's instructions in verse ten with Daniel's instructions in Daniel 12:4

10) Explain the message of Revelation 22:11. In your explanation, make a connection with verse 15.

Discussion:

How well do you know the Bible? Without aid of scriptural direction, explain verse sixteen as to Jesus' relation to David regarding linage and Kingship.

11) What is the final warning concerning the Book of Revelation?

12) How do you explain to a scoffer *"I am coming soon?"* See Overview

Summary Statement:

This chapter is the summation of two trees. The first is described in Genesis 2-3. It is also the conclusion of God's mission on earth in the person of Jesus. (Matthew 10:32-39) Eternal bliss is the destiny for those who positioned Christ first in their life while destruction awaits those who made other choices. <u>John's final epilogue is for men to keep God's Word unaltered</u>. The Bible began with God in control and it closes with Him in control. In the end, those who wanted Jesus get their wish and those who didn't want Him get their wish also!

"Blessed is he who keeps the words of the prophecy in this book."

Composer Johannes Brahms said of the subject of this chapter, *'How lovely is Thy dwelling-place. Blessed are they in Thy house that dwell.'* Brahms words contradict those who believe that when you are dead you are dead and that's all there is. O' how tragic to think the place described in these final two chapters does not exist! It means no plans were made beyond this life! What is described here *is* available. How foolish to reject it! Those who take God at His Word can anticipate an unbelievable existence awaits them. *"These words are trustworthy and true."*

In our study of these closing chapters and the Bible as a whole, let us not overanalyze the Scriptures but simply let God say what He wants to say. Those who spiritualize these final two chapters unwittingly diminish the power of God first displayed in Genesis and revealed throughout Scripture. Everything we see and experience today, science and its laws, God spoke into existence! Will not this same power create what is described here? God will not lose His touch! Certainly the science of which we are familiar will be changed.

Chapter twenty-one described the geography and architecture of the Holy City. Here John describes the provisions of the city. Verse two provides information from which we can draw some conclusions. We already know the Holy City is home for Christ and His Church. The Jews have uncontested dominion over the land about the city given them in the Old Testament. Non-church sheep make up the nations. Clearly, nourishment is centered here. Not only for those living in the city, but those living around the city and across the nations. John's use of the term monthly suggests all inhabitants require scheduled regeneration. Just as the city will be a center for worship, it also is a supermarket, power and water supply. The Boeing 737 will be replaced with the same method of travel found in Matthew 28:9-10, Mark 16:12, Luke 24:15-31, 36-52, John 20:14-17, 19, 26. These are not examples of passing through doors like a ghost, but they do reveal a science Jesus has already made use of. The ability to relocate.

Application

Warren Wiersbe says of these closing chapters, "heaven is more than a destination; it is a motivation." Knowing that one day you and I shall dwell in the heavenly city has to make a difference in our lives here and now." *"Blessed are those who wash their robes, that they may have the right to the tree of life and may go through the gates into the city."* Is Christ Jesus the Cornerstone of your life? Beloved, if you have not received Jesus, do so where you sit. Pray this prayer; 'Lord, I am lost. I am helpless to save myself. I place my trust in You and rejoice at calling You my Lord and my Savior.' Amen

Glossary of Imagery by Verse for Revelation 22

v. 1	river - water of life	God's provision to sustain Eternal life - coincides with God providing a river of water in the Garden of Eden
v. 2	tree of life	provides monthly nutrition - Monthly production does suggest a form of time will exist. Revelation 21:25 indicates time is measured although night is not dark. This would indicate sleep is either absent or rest is not rest as we know it.
v. 3	leaves - healing	suggests an ounce of prevention is worth a pound of cure
v. 3	curse	Sin will not exist or will it ever. Recall sin did reappear at the end of the Millennial Kingdom for a brief time to test those born during a time of perfect conditions until the re-release of Satan. (Revelation 20:7) This would suggest there is no more reproduction.
v. 7	soon	If you are puzzled by the meaning of soon, this means at the onset of Daniel's seventieth week, (Tribulation) Christ will return in seven years or one week of years. Soon has nothing to do with the Church-Age we are currently in.
v. 14	wash their robes	To be washed in the Blood of the Lamb carries the blessing of Eternal life.
v. 17	Spirit - Bride	The Third person of the Trinity and the Church which is the Home of the Spirit invite all sinners who will listen to Salvation.
v. 21	Amen	use here - confirm the solemn Covenant of this Prophecy

Notes for Revelation 22

Woe to those who call evil good

and good evil.

Who put darkness for light

and light for darkness.

Who put bitter for sweet

and sweet for bitter.

Woe to those who are wise in their own eyes

and clever in their own sight.

Woe to those who are heroes at drinking wine

and champions at mixing drinks,

who acquit the guilty for a bribe,

but deny justice to the innocent.

Isaiah 5:20-23

Blessed are they who wash their robes

That they may have the right

To the tree of life.

And may go through the gates

Into the city.

I am the Alpha and the Omega

The First and the Last

The Beginning and the End

CONCLUDING DISSERTATION

"Now all has been heard; Fear God and keep His commandments, for this is the whole duty of man."
"For God will bring every deed into judgment, including every hidden thing, whether it is good or evil."
Ecclesiastes 12:13-14

God is in control! The world is going to be corrected. The meek will inherit the earth. Judgment is certain. Since the foundation of the world, God has crafted a plan for those who love Him and those who ignore Him. The works of men will be thrown down; its cities, its authorities, its values will be overturned. With the Second Coming, the pronouncement of the Lord's Prayer will be fulfilled. *"Your kingdom come, "your will be done, on earth."* Words cannot describe the world God plans for His own. *"They will be his people, and God himself will be with them."* And all the earth will live by *"the eternal gospel."* (Revelation 14) There *will* be peace on earth.

Isaiah, whose name means the Lord saves, foretold of God's plan to send Jesus into the world to save all who would receive Him. Isaiah describes Jesus using a familiar element; snow. Snow has beauty, its property is water. John's vision fulfills Isaiah's prophecy. *"Then the angel showed me the river of the water of life."* (Revelation 22:1) Coming from above, Jesus is like the snow, free of earthly contamination.

<u>Because of where Jesus is today, there is hope for tomorrow.</u> These two studies are a look into a joyous future that assures a time is coming when selfish appetites, violent men and all manner of lasciviousness are as extinct as are the dinosaurs. That glorious day when Christ our Lord reigns from Zion. Marantha!

"He will reign on David's throne and over his kingdom, establishing and upholding it with justice and righteousness from that time on and forever."
Isaiah 9:7

SIN

A man cannot say he loves the Lord and persist in doing the works of the devil.

The backdrop of sin began with <u>two trees</u>. Obedience and rebellion; life and death, centered on two trees. As in Genesis, it is quite apparent today, the craftiness of the devil has enticed men to eat fruit from whatever tree it pleases them.

Beloved, Let us not be found among those who bend and twist God's Word seeking loopholes to justify what we already know in our heart is plainly sin.

Just as it was in the days of Noah,
So also will it be in the days of the Son of Man. (The Church Age)
People were eating, drinking, marrying
And being given in marriage
Up to the day Noah entered the ark. (Rapture)
Then the flood came and destroyed them all."

"It was in the days of Lot. (Facsimile of the Church Age)
People were eating and drinking,
Buying and selling, planning and building.
But the day Lot left Sodom, (Facsimile of Rapture)
Fire and sulfur rained down from heaven
And destroyed them all."

Luke 17:26-29

<u>Sin is the problem!</u> Sin in our modern culture is not cool, consequently, the culture's influence weakens the Church on the subject. Reluctant to offend its base, the Church takes a more antiseptic approach. "Sins are those things other people commit." Would it be unfair to say the average church goer is more attuned to the coming new I-phone than the coming Judgment? Both Revelation 2 and 3 and 1 Peter 4:17 call for an awareness of sin right under our nose.

If sin is not fully distinguished, then how pray-tell do we avoid the devil's deceptions?

Might not we be wise to advance beyond the usual suspects of adultery and gossip; expressly, deceptive sins that entangle people in the devil's traps? *"Your enemy the devil prowls around like a roaring lion seeking someone to devour."* (1 Peter 5:8) The foregoing are two issues of our time. On one, the Church seems firm; the other, the Church is noticeably silent and that is troubling.

Downward

God's original plan was for men to live by His laws but men had other ideas. <u>To live to please self</u>. God tested Adam's resolve to obedience and He tests us today. It is naïve to believe the devil isn't allowed to test us. Faith, like any muscle, needs exercise. Secondly, God is glorified by the resolve of His people to resist the devil's arrows. God was glorified when Jesus and Job withstood the devil's temptations. Adam and Eve were defeated by the devil because they chose to have their way!

Still, the creation of Adam and Eve are testimonies to God's creative genius. The union of male and female <u>established marriage</u>, <u>ordained physical love</u> and <u>ordered procreation</u>. Deceived by the devil, some resort to ambiguity to justify same-sex marriage by using love as a loophole. They assert if love is present, God, being love, surely blesses same-sex marriage. No matter how ambitious the ambiguity, proclaiming same-sex marital-union equal to a Holy God's plan is fraught with peril.

Here's the problem. Same-sex marriage is a carbon-copy of Adam and Eve's decision to <u>have their way</u>. *"There is a way that seems right to a man, but in the end it leads to death."* (Proverbs 14:12) <u>Man's way never glorifies God</u>. God's creative genius goes unrecognized in that, same-sex marriage cannot procreate. *"Be fruitful and multiply."* (Genesis 1:28) Same-sex intimacy fails to glorify God! Beloved, those on board with this rebellion are on board with the devil. *"Women exchanged natural relations for unnatural ones. In the same way men abandoned natural relations with women and were inflamed with lust for one another. Men committed indecent acts with other men."* (Romans 1:26-27) Clearly, Jesus was not redefining marriage when He recited Genesis 2. *"At the beginning of creation, God made them male and female and the two will become <u>one flesh</u>."* (Mark 10:6-8) What is there not to understand here? Song of Solomon gives further evidence.

"Woe to those who call evil good."

Delusion

"Even the smartest among us can succumb to periods of collective madness, in
which people cannot see what is right in front of their very eyes."
William Falk

William Falk is not a Theologian but might we affix madness to propagating sin? There was a time a youngster's trouble with a teacher put him in trouble at home. Trouble at home was replaced with, "my dad will beat you up!" Then came, "our lawyer will sue the school!" Now, in this unfolding age of the gun, dads and lawyers are antiquated. Profiteers have provided sophisticated weaponry to settle grievances.

Sophisticated gunnery is the golden calf of some. Ambiguous claims are made to attach weaponry to the Divine. These misguided souls have much in common with Cervantes' character; I, Don Quixote. A syndrome where by, one is accomplishing just the opposite of what he believes he is accomplishing. Promises of safety and security these weapons would bring have not panned out. Rather, what is liberty for one man is the end of life, liberty and the pursuit of happiness for scores of others.

Amazingly, some who vehemently oppose abortion are at microphones championing distribution of battle-field weaponry among civilian society. Is this not hypocrisy? Battlefield weapons are sold as one sells roadside vegetables. Is this not madness? Undoubtedly, the instrument to commit mass murder is as close as a friend's house. And, the proliferation of such weapons is called virtuous by some!

Is sin present in this, and if so, who is guilty; the perpetrators, the facilitators, the profiteers? Assuredly, a Holy God will hold enablers of murder just as accountable as the perpetrators. (Matthew 18:7) The Holiness of the Lord cannot dictate otherwise.

"Political issue, not moral," say some! Oh how Matthew 18:7 and 2 Peter 2:17-19 refute such a view. Is morality a matter of appetite? Can we not sacrifice something here? Isn't sacrifice at the heart of love? My friend, had Jesus not made the sacrifice He did, you and I would be in a real fix! If we are a disciple of Christ, let us not be hypocritical when we stand and sing, *I surrender all.* (Except my AR 15)

Whatever thrills them, desperate men will say or do anything to preserve their pleasurable excitements. Often passive-aggressive, these souls see self as the center of the universe. They easily assume the role of victim when opposed. They consider anyone opposing them enemies of freedom and even of God. They align themselves with power at the expense of the helpless. Paul's writing on the subject of selfishness makes this relevant for Bible study. *"Do nothing out of selfish ambition, but in humility consider others better than yourselves. Each of you should look not only to your own interests, but also to the interests of others."* Beloved, the children of Sandy Hook were executed by a battlefield weapon. Time has passed but nothing has changed. Wonderfully, the Church defends the unborn. Isn't it time the Church defends the born? Are they not both moral and biblical issues? (Philippians 2:3-4)

The unfolding idolatry of guns and advanced weaponry in one respect is biblical. *"Then another horse came out, a fiery red horse. Its rider was given power to take peace from the earth and to make men slay each other."* (Revelation 6:4)

Technology has advanced but men have not. Sixty plus countries are engaged in armed conflict every day. Societal strife is endless. All the result of prideful men about their daily business of self. Arrogance defines them. Peace with God is elusive because having their way is their peace! Even in meaningless situations they delight in taking rather than giving, winning rather than relinquishing. They refuse to die to self. Such is the way of Cain. *"Anyone who does not carry his cross and follow me cannot be my disciple."* (Luke 14:27)

Whatever the ambiguity lustful men disseminate, all are bedfellows in sin and a <u>Holy God is going to Judge the lot of it</u>. Let us pray for God to raise up gritty expositors who aren't afraid to call owning an arsenal idol worship.

When appetites displace knowledge, sin is not far behind.

Rebellion

Billy Graham's name appeared in this workbook as one who associated himself with nearly a dozen presidents of differing political persuasions. It was apparent, Mr. Graham was an ambassador of Christ and never framed as a voice for a political ideology. By this, thousands of souls from varying political persuasions came to know Jesus. Observing the climate at the preparation of this book, ambassadorship of the Church has become blurred depending on one's geography and political persuasion. Where Mr. Graham brought people together, divisiveness has taken root. The bitter fruit of this error is Christ becomes the possession of a political ideology. This is the same sort of covetousness ancient Israel engaged in.

Debasing the President of the United States is applauded in some Congregations. Is this not suggestive of Korah's rebellion? With church people proactive in the internet frenzy to hate a sitting president, we have to take note. This has led some to believe armed defiance of government authority or precipitating violence against its institutions is serving God.

Rebellion to God's Sovereignty over nations is a serious thing. *"The Lord is good to those <u>whose hope is in him</u>. It is good to wait quietly for the salvation of the Lord."* (Lamentations 3:25-26) Waiting on the Lord means man is not to call the shots. The consequences of this self-indulgent thinking is Divine Judgment. One only need examine Numbers Sixteen to know this truth. Expositors must spell it out to some folks! <u>There is a greater purpose than one nation, one leader</u>. Judging from the news, Romans 13:1-2 and 1 Peter 2:13-17 seem to be missing from some Bibles.

Beloved, whoever is President of these United States, he, like all leaders, are God's men to orchestrate a portion of the coming Judgment conveyed by Daniel and John.

A church that never addresses the subject of sin and rebellion must surely be filled with perfect people.

Unselfish Thinking

Humility is at the heart of unselfish thinking. This begins with coming to terms with what we think we are entitled to. Beloved, we are all entitled to hell. Mercifully, God has rescued us. Humility doesn't have to be difficult. Norman Vincent Peale and Ken Blanchard say it best; "people with humility don't think less of themselves; they just think of themselves less." The writings of the Apostle Paul on the subject of humility articulate how God humbled Himself. He removed His crown, left the glory of heaven and came down to earth as a Man. He humbled Himself to unjust condemnation by wicked men. He finished humility's work by being nailed to a tree.

"Blessed is the man
  Who does not walk in the counsel
    Of the wicked." Psalm 1:1

Printed in the United States
By Bookmasters